THE YOSEMITE

John Muir's remarkable early career as mountaineer, explorer and student of nature in the ranges of California was followed by another which brought him wide fame and influence as the Nation's foremost park and wilderness conservationist. Authorship was secondary to him, and his first book did not appear until he was past fifty. But the charm, vigor and descriptive accuracy of his autobiographical writings, his chapters on forests, glaciers and mountain beauty in the Far West and Alaska, and his sympathetic accounts of the water ouzel and the dog Stickeen, have been read and enjoyed for more than seven decades. Born in Scotland in 1838, he spent his boyhood on a Wisconsin farm, attended the University of Wisconsin, wandered in Canada, the South, and Cuba, then found his way to his promised land in California. He lived in Yosemite almost continuously from 1868 to 1873, and visited the area frequently in later years. He was a gifted amateur naturalist and made important observations in geology and glaciology. His conservation campaigns led to the establishment of Federal forest reserves, Yosemite and Sequoia National Parks, and eventually the National Park System. He died on Christmas Eve in 1914.

The Yosemite was first published in 1912 by The Century Co.

Hetch Hetchy

SIERRA

Tioga Pass

TUOLUMNE RIVER

Mt. Dana

Mt. Hoffman

TUOLUMNE
MEADOWS

Tenaya
Lake

NEVADA

BIG TREES

BIG TREES

Yosemite
Valley

Half Dome

MERCED RIVER

Mt. Lyell

Mt. Clark

MARIPOSA
BIG TREES

N

CALIFORNIA

Area
of map

0   5   10 MILES

Yosemite
National Park

CALIFORNIA

THE YOSEMITE

BY

JOHN MUIR

With Notes and an Introduction by
FREDERIC R. GUNSKY

PUBLISHED IN CO-OPERATION WITH
THE AMERICAN MUSEUM OF NATURAL HISTORY

THE NATURAL HISTORY LIBRARY
ANCHOR BOOKS
DOUBLEDAY & COMPANY, INC.
GARDEN CITY, NEW YORK

The Yosemite was originally published by The Century Company in 1912. The Natural History Library edition is published by arrangement with Appleton-Century-Crofts Trade Books.

Natural History Library edition with Notes and an Introduction by Frederic R. Gunsky: 1962

Maps prepared by Walter Rivers and drawn by Stephen Kraft.

CONTENTS

ACKNOWLEDGMENT

On the early history of Yosemite the writer is indebted to Prof. J. D. Whitney for quotations from his volume entitled "Yosemite Guide-Book," and to Dr. Bunnell for extracts from his interesting volume entitled "Discovery of the Yosemite."

INTRODUCTION

In 1912, just after John Muir completed this "guide-book" for walkers and the carriage trade, the Honorable Secretary of the Interior called a National Parks conference in Yosemite Valley. The great question, Muir wrote to the secretary of the American Alpine Club, was "Shall automobiles be allowed to enter Yosemite?"

"A prodigious lot of gaseous commercial eloquence was spent upon it," the patriarch of conservation observed. He conceded that all signs indicated victory for the autos, which had previously been prohibited, officially by regulations and unofficially by steep grades. "Doubtless, under certain precautionary restrictions, these useful, progressive, blunt-nosed mechanical beetles will hereafter be allowed to puff their way into all the parks and mingle their gas-breath with the breath of the pines and waterfalls, and, from the mountaineer's standpoint, with but little harm or good."

The next year, cars began entering the Valley via the Coulterville Road. They were permitted to speed ten miles an hour on "rolling mountain country," fifteen on the Valley floor; in all, 127 of them were admitted during the season. In 1914, the year Muir died, civilian administrators took over from the U. S. Army, and Wawona Road and Big Oak Flat Road were opened to motor traffic. The modern era of the National Parks had begun.

Fifty years have passed since *The Yosemite* was first published. The population of the United States has doubled, leisure time has pyramided, and travel has been revolutionized. During 1961, some 1,227,110 persons visited Yosemite. The budget submitted by the President to Congress for the 1963 fiscal year provided nearly two million dollars for construction in the Park, half of it allotted directly to road building. Muir, who deprecated the fact that "most visitors have to be rolled on wheels with blankets and kitchen arrangements," might have wished to reconsider whether the mechanical beetles did but little harm.

Chapters of this handbook for travelers remain, like those of *The Mountains of California, My First Summer in the Sierra,* and *Our National Parks,* true classics of personal discovery and reverence for nature. The volume describes important features of a 1200-square-mile high-country preserve which relatively few Americans of the free-wheeling decades have penetrated beyond the roadheads. Yosemite liberated the best in Muir, from his first glimpse of the peaks and streams and the incomparable Valley in 1868, when he was thirty, to the exhausting battle for Hetch Hetchy which he lost nearly a half-century afterward. *The Yosemite* is a distillation of those years, the singular, forceful expression of two personalities—Muir's and the land's. John Muir was Yosemite's finest guide, and his book is practical. The uninitiated reader nevertheless needs an occasional bit of advice or caution. Fifty years of "development" have wrought changes in modes of travel, facilities, and access to various places. Scientific investigation has improved the knowledge of land forms and their history (although Fritiof Fryxell says Muir became "more intimately familiar with the facts and more nearly right in their interpretation than any professional geologist of his time"). Common names of some flora and fauna, even generic and specific names, have been modified. A few of Muir's place names must be explained. The footnotes provided in this edition are intended, not to correct the text, but to help the reader follow the lucid prose of an author who cared much for accuracy as well as beauty.

Because discretion is an acknowledged part of valor, the chapter on "How Best to Spend One's Yosemite Time" requires comment. Muir was long-legged, intensely energetic and, when he was in the mountains, oblivious of creature comforts. Carrying nothing but a little flour, tea and sugar, he seemed to stride across the high country in seven-league boots. Few of us travel as fast or as tirelessly, so it has been considered prudent to indicate, after each recommended excursion, just how many trail miles are involved. Most readers, until they have tested themselves in the Sierra, should not attempt to cover the distance in the time Muir suggests.

Saddest of the footnotes are those appended to the chapter on beautiful Hetch Hetchy Valley, which was invaded not by automobiles but by a water and power project that Muir fought bitterly. His most effective weapon was his public utterances, including this book. "Dam Hetch Hetchy!" he exclaimed. "As well dam for water-tanks the people's cathedrals and churches, for no holier temple has ever been consecrated by the heart of man."

Conservationists lost their campaign to prevent the damming of the Tuolumne River inside Yosemite National Park. The City of San Francisco, which could as well have impounded water elsewhere, began construction activities just before Muir died—of a broken heart, it has been said. Ansel Adams, who alone portrays Yosemite with equal authority, can never practice his photographic art in the Hetch Hetchy that Muir knew, the sister "yosemite" whose fate it was to be a tragic object lesson.

But do not be misled. *The Yosemite* is a joyous book, a guide to a land of eternal youth. Although written by a man in his seventies who had arranged "old musty dusty Yosemite notes . . . in something like lateral, medial, and terminal moraines on my den floor," it is redolent of bright sunshine and the odor of pines in clean mountain air. It recalls days of exuberant pleasure in the sights and sounds of an almost untouched wilderness. Through Muir's words the trees and flowers become eloquent, storms and earthquakes echo, the vital spirit of tough juniper and fierce golden eagle finds expression. Not sentimentally but with sensitivity and awe, he carries us to the heart of sequoia groves, waterfalls, river canyons and the granite high country of the Range of Light.

Despite the millions of visitors with their autos, the chief park values of which Muir was a great interpreter are still there to be rediscovered by each generation. The Sierra Club, other conservation groups, and the National Park Service, all of which had their origins in Muir's efforts, willingly share the burden of protecting these scenic treasures. He would urge you, because the grandeur is still there, to accept this invitation and go discover for yourself.

Frederic R. Gunsky

28 January 1962
Mill Valley, California

Assistance of the following is gratefully acknowledged: Douglass H. Hubbard, Chief Park Naturalist, Yosemite Park; Robert P. Howell, San Rafael; Dr. Carl W. Sharsmith, San Jose State College.

F.R.G.

I

THE APPROACH TO THE VALLEY

When I set out on the long excursion that finally led to California I wandered afoot and alone, from Indiana to the Gulf of Mexico, with a plant-press on my back, holding a generally southward course, like the birds when they are going from summer to winter. From the west coast of Florida I crossed the gulf to Cuba, enjoyed the rich tropical flora there for a few months, intending to go thence to the north end of South America, make my way through the woods to the headwaters of the Amazon, and float down that grand river to the ocean. But I was unable to find a ship bound for South America—fortunately perhaps, for I had incredibly little money for so long a trip and had not yet fully recovered from a fever caught in the Florida swamps. Therefore I decided to visit California for a year or two to see its wonderful flora and the famous Yosemite Valley. All the world was before me and every day was a holiday, so it did not seem important to which one of the world's wildernesses I first should wander.

Arriving by the Panama steamer, I stopped one day in San Francisco and then inquired for the nearest way out of town. "But where do you want to go?" asked the man to whom I had applied for this important information. "To any place that is wild," I said. This reply startled him. He seemed to fear I might be crazy and therefore the sooner I was out of town the better, so he directed me to the Oakland ferry.

So on the first of April, 1868, I set out afoot for Yosemite. It was the bloom-time of the year over the lowlands and coast ranges; the landscapes of the Santa
Clara Valley were fairly drenched with sunshine, all
the air was quivering with the songs of the meadow-
larks, and the hills were so covered with flowers that
they seemed to be painted. Slow indeed was my progress through these glorious gardens, the first of the
California flora I had seen. Cattle and cultivation were
making few scars as yet, and I wandered enchanted
in long wavering curves, knowing by my pocket map
that Yosemite Valley lay to the east and that I should
surely find it.

THE SIERRA FROM THE WEST

Looking eastward from the summit of the Pacheco
Pass one shining morning, a landscape was displayed
that after all my wanderings still appears as the most
beautiful I have ever beheld. At my feet lay the Great
Central Valley of California, level and flowery, like a
lake of pure sunshine, forty or fifty miles wide, five
hundred miles long, one rich furred garden of yellow
Compositæ. And from the eastern boundary of this
vast golden flower-bed rose the mighty Sierra, miles in
height, and so gloriously colored and so radiant, it
seemed not clothed with light, but wholly composed
of it, like the wall of some celestial city. Along the top
and extending a good way down, was a rich pearl-gray
belt of snow; below it a belt of blue and dark purple,
marking the extension of the forests; and stretching
along the base of the range a broad belt of rose-purple; all these colors, from the blue sky to the yellow
valley smoothly blending as they do in a rainbow,
making a wall of light ineffably fine. Then it seemed
to me that the Sierra should be called, not the Nevada
or Snowy Range, but the Range of Light. And after

ten years of wandering and wondering in the heart of it, rejoicing in its glorious floods of light, the white beams of the morning streaming through the passes, the noonday radiance on the crystal rocks, the flush of the alpenglow, and the irised spray of countless waterfalls, it still seems above all others the Range of Light.

In general views no mark of man is visible upon it, nor anything to suggest the wonderful depth and grandeur of its sculpture. None of its magnificent forest-crowned ridges seems to rise much above the general level to publish its wealth. No great valley or river is seen, or group of well-marked features of any kind standing out as distinct pictures. Even the summit peaks, marshaled in glorious array so high in the sky, seem comparatively regular in form. Nevertheless the whole range five hundred miles long is furrowed with canyons 2000 to 5000 feet deep, in which once flowed majestic glaciers, and in which now flow and sing the bright rejoicing rivers.

CHARACTERISTICS OF THE CANYONS

Though of such stupendous depth, these canyons are not gloomy gorges, savage and inaccessible. With rough passages here and there they are flowery pathways conducting to the snowy, icy fountains; mountain streets full of life and light, graded and sculptured by the ancient glaciers, and presenting throughout all their courses a rich variety of novel and attractive scenery—the most attractive that has yet been discovered in the mountain ranges of the world. In many places, especially in the middle region of the western flank, the main canyons widen into spacious valleys or parks diversified like landscape gardens with meadows and groves and thickets of blooming bushes, while the lofty walls, infinitely varied in form, are fringed with ferns, flowering plants, shrubs of many species, and tall evergreens and oaks that find footholds on small benches and tables, all enlivened and made glorious with rejoicing streams that come chanting in chorus over the cliffs and through side canyons in falls of every conceivable form, to join the river that flows in tranquil, shining beauty down the middle of each one of them.

THE INCOMPARABLE YOSEMITE

The most famous and accessible of these canyon valleys, and also the one that presents their most striking and sublime features on the grandest scale, is the Yosemite, situated in the basin of the Merced River at an elevation of 4000 feet above the level of the sea. It is about seven miles long, half a mile to a mile wide, and nearly a mile deep in the solid granite flank of the range. The walls are made up of rocks, mountains in size, partly separated from each other by side canyons, and they are so sheer in front, and so compactly and harmoniously arranged on a level floor, that the Valley, comprehensively seen, looks like an immense hall or temple lighted from above.

But no temple made with hands can compare with Yosemite. Every rock in its walls seems to glow with life. Some lean back in majestic repose; others, absolutely sheer or nearly so for thousands of feet, advance beyond their companions in thoughtful attitudes, giving welcome to storms and calms alike, seemingly aware, yet heedless, of everything going on about them. Awful in stern, immovable majesty, how softly these rocks are adorned, and how fine and reassuring the company they keep: their feet among beautiful groves and meadows, their brows in the sky, a thousand flowers leaning confidingly against their feet, bathed in floods of water, floods of light, while the

snow and waterfalls, the winds and avalanches and
clouds shine and sing and wreathe about them as the
years go by, and myriads of small winged creatures—
birds, bees, butterflies—give glad animation and help
to make all the air into music. Down through the middle of the Valley flows the crystal Merced, River of
Mercy, peacefully quiet, reflecting lilies and trees and
the onlooking rocks; things frail and fleeting and types
of endurance meeting here and blending in countless
forms, as if into this one mountain mansion Nature had
gathered her choicest treasures, to draw her lovers into
close and confiding communion with her.

THE APPROACH TO THE VALLEY

Sauntering up the foothills to Yosemite by any of
the old trails or roads in use before the railway was
built from the town of Merced up the river to the
boundary of Yosemite Park, richer and wilder become
the forests and streams. At an elevation of 6000 feet
above the level of the sea the silver firs are 200 feet
high, with branches whorled around the colossal shafts
in regular order, and every branch beautifully pinnate
like a fern frond. The Douglas spruce,[1] the yellow and
sugar pines and brown-barked libocedrus here reach
their finest developments of beauty and grandeur. The
majestic sequoia is here, too, the king of conifers, the
noblest of all the noble race. These colossal trees are as
wonderful in fineness of beauty and proportion as in
stature—an assemblage of conifers surpassing all that
have ever yet been discovered in the forests of the
world. Here indeed is the tree-lover's paradise; the
woods, dry and wholesome, letting in the light in shimmering masses of half sunshine, half shade; the night
air as well as the day air indescribably spicy and ex-

[1] Douglas fir, *Pseudotsuga taxifolia.*

hilarating; plushy fir-boughs for campers' beds, and
cascades to sing us to sleep. On the highest ridges, over
which these old Yosemite ways passed, the silver fir
(*Abies magnifica*) forms the bulk of the woods, pressing forward in glorious array to the very brink of the
Valley walls on both sides, and beyond the Valley to
a height of from 8000 to 9000 feet above the level of
the sea. Thus it appears that Yosemite, presenting such
stupendous faces of bare granite, is nevertheless imbedded in magnificent forests, and the main species of
pine, fir, spruce and libocedrus are also found in the
Valley itself, but there are no "big trees" (*Sequoia
gigantea*) in the Valley or about the rim of it. The
nearest are about ten and twenty miles beyond the
lower end of the Valley on small tributaries of the
Merced and Tuolumne Rivers.

THE FIRST VIEW: THE BRIDAL VEIL

From the margin of these glorious forests the first
general view of the Valley used to be gained—a revela-
tion in landscape affairs that enriches one's life forever.
Entering the Valley, gazing overwhelmed with the
multitude of grand objects about us, perhaps the first
to fix our attention will be the Bridal Veil, a beautiful
waterfall on our right. Its brow, where it first leaps free
from the cliff, is about 900 feet above us; and as it
sways and sings in the wind, clad in gauzy, sun-sifted
spray, half falling, half floating, it seems infinitely gentle and fine; but the hymns it sings tell the solemn fate-
ful power hidden beneath its soft clothing.

The Bridal Veil shoots free from the upper edge of
the cliff by the velocity the stream has acquired in descending a long slope above the head of the fall. Looking from the top of the rock-avalanche talus on the
west side, about one hundred feet above the foot of
the fall, the under surface of the water arch is seen

to be finely grooved and striated; and the sky is seen through the arch between rock and water, making a novel and beautiful effect.

Under ordinary weather conditions the fall strikes on flat-topped slabs, forming a kind of ledge about two-thirds of the way down from the top, and as the fall sways back and forth with great variety of motions among these flat-topped pillars, kissing and plashing notes as well as thunder-like detonations are produced, like those of the Yosemite Fall, though on a smaller scale.

The rainbows of the Veil, or rather the spray- and foam-bows, are superb, because the waters are dashed among angular blocks of granite at the foot, producing abundance of spray of the best quality for iris effects, and also for a luxuriant growth of grass and maidenhair on the side of the talus, which lower down is planted with oak, laurel and willows.

GENERAL FEATURES OF THE VALLEY

On the other side of the Valley, almost immediately opposite the Bridal Veil, there is another fine fall, considerably wider than the Veil when the snow is melting fast and more than 1000 feet in height, measured from the brow of the cliff where it first springs out into the air to the head of the rocky talus on which it strikes and is broken up into ragged cascades. It is called the Ribbon Fall or Virgin's Tears. During the spring floods it is a magnificent object, but the suffocating blasts of spray that fill the recess in the wall which it occupies prevent a near approach. In autumn, however, when its feeble current falls in a shower, it may then pass for tears with the sentimental onlooker fresh from a visit to the Bridal Veil.

Just beyond this glorious flood the El Capitan Rock, regarded by many as the most sublime feature of the

Half Dome

Nevada Fall

Vernal Fall

TENAYA CREEK

Mirror Lake

Basket Dome

North Dome

MERCED RIVER

Glacier Point

Sentinel Dome

Sentinel Rock

Yosemite Falls

Three Brothers
Eagle Peak

N

Cathedral Spires

El Capitan

CALIFORNIA

Area of map

Bridalveil Fall

Yosemite Valley

0   1   2 MILES

Valley, is seen through the pine groves, standing forward beyond the general line of the wall in most imposing grandeur, a type of permanence. It is 3300 feet high, a plain, severely simple, glacier-sculptured face of granite, the end of one of the most compact and enduring of the mountain ridges, unrivaled in height and breadth and flawless strength.

Across the Valley from here, next to the Bridal Veil, are the picturesque Cathedral Rocks, nearly 2700 feet high, making a noble display of fine yet massive sculpture. They are closely related to El Capitan, having been eroded from the same mountain ridge by the great Yosemite Glacier when the Valley was in process of formation.

Next to the Cathedral Rocks on the south side towers the Sentinel Rock to a height of more than 3000 feet, a telling monument of the glacial period.

Almost immediately opposite the Sentinel are the Three Brothers, an immense mountain mass with three gables fronting the Valley, one above another, the topmost gable nearly 4000 feet high. They were named for three brothers, sons of old Tenaya, the Yosemite chief, captured here during the Indian War, at the time of the discovery of the Valley in 1851.

Sauntering up the Valley through meadow and grove, in the company of these majestic rocks, which seem to follow us as we advance, gazing, admiring, looking for new wonders ahead where all about us is so wonderful, the thunder of the Yosemite Fall is heard, and when we arrive in front of the Sentinel Rock it is revealed in all its glory from base to summit, half a mile in height, and seeming to spring out into the Valley sunshine direct from the sky. But even this fall, perhaps the most wonderful of its kind in the world, cannot at first hold our attention, for now the wide upper portion of the Valley is displayed to

view, with the finely modeled North Dome, the Royal
Arches and Washington Column on our left; Glacier
Point, with its massive, magnificent sculpture on the
right; and in the middle, directly in front, looms Tissiack or Half Dome, the most beautiful and most sublime of all the wonderful Yosemite rocks, rising in
serene majesty from flowery groves and meadows to a
height of 4750 feet.

THE UPPER CANYONS

Here the Valley divides into three branches, the
Tenaya, Nevada, and Illilouette Canyons, extending
back into the fountains of the High Sierra, with scenery every way worthy the relation they bear to Yosemite.

In the south branch, a mile or two from the main
Valley, is the Illilouette Fall, 600 feet high, one of the
most beautiful of all the Yosemite choir, but to most
people inaccessible as yet on account of its rough,
steep, boulder-choked canyon.[2] Its principal fountains
of ice and snow lie in the beautiful and interesting
mountains of the Merced group, while its broad open
basin between its fountain mountains and canyon is
noted for the beauty of its lakes and forests and magnificent moraines.

Returning to the Valley, and going up the north
branch of Tenaya Canyon, we pass between the North
Dome and Half Dome, and in less than an hour come
to Mirror Lake, the Dome Cascades,[3] and Tenaya Fall.
Beyond the Fall, on the north side of the canyon, is
the sublime El Capitan-like rock called Mount Watkins; on the south the vast granite wave of Clouds
Rest, a mile in height; and between them the fine

[2] Illilouette Fall is reached by trail from Glacier Point or
Nevada Fall.
[3] Probably the cascade down the side of Basket Dome.

Tenaya Cascade with silvery plumes outspread on smooth glacier-polished folds of granite, making a vertical descent in all of about 700 feet.

Just beyond the Dome Cascades, on the shoulder of Mount Watkins, there is an old trail once used by Indians on their way across the range to Mono, but in the canyon above this point there is no trail of any sort. Between Mount Watkins and Clouds Rest the canyon is accessible only to mountaineers, and it is so dangerous that I hesitate to advise even good climbers, anxious to test their nerve and skill, to attempt to pass through it.[4] Beyond the Cascades no great difficulty will be encountered. A succession of charming lily gardens and meadows occurs in filled-up lake basins among the rock-waves in the bottom of the canyon, and everywhere the surface of the granite has a smooth-wiped appearance, and in many places reflects the sunbeams like glass, a phenomenon due to glacial action, the canyon having been the channel of one of the main tributaries of the ancient Yosemite Glacier.

About ten miles above the Valley we come to the beautiful Tenaya Lake, and here the canyon terminates. A mile or two above the lake stands the grand Sierra Cathedral,[5] a building of one stone, hewn from the living rock, with sides, roof, gable, spire and ornamental pinnacles, fashioned and finished symmetrically like a work of art, and set on a well-graded plateau about 9000 feet high, as if Nature in making so fine a building had also been careful that it should be finely seen. From every direction its peculiar form and graceful, majestic beauty of expression never fail to

[4] There is still no trail up Tenaya Creek, although one has been proposed. One mile above Mirror Lake, the Tenaya Lake and Soda Springs Trail begins its zigzag course up the mountainside opposite Half Dome. A spur trail goes on a half-mile to Snow Creek Fall.
[5] Cathedral Peak, elevation 10,933.

charm. Its height from its base to the ridge of the roof
is about 2500 feet, and among the pinnacles that adorn
the front grand views may be gained of the upper
basins of the Merced and Tuolumne Rivers.

Passing the Cathedral we descend into the delightful, spacious Tuolumne Valley, from which excursions
may be made to Mounts Dana, Lyell, Ritter, Conness,
and Mono Lake, and to the many curious peaks that
rise above the meadows on the south, and to the Big
Tuolumne Canyon, with its glorious abundance of
rocks and falling, gliding, tossing water. For all these
the beautiful meadows near the Soda Springs form a
delightful center.

NATURAL FEATURES NEAR THE VALLEY

Returning now to Yosemite and ascending the middle or Nevada branch of the Valley, occupied by the
main Merced River, we come within a few miles to
the Vernal and Nevada Falls, 400 and 600 feet high,
pouring their white, rejoicing waters in the midst of
the most novel and sublime rock scenery to be found
in all the world. Tracing the river beyond the head of
the Nevada Fall we are led into the Little Yosemite,
a valley like the great Yosemite in form, sculpture and
vegetation. It is about three miles long, with walls
1500 to 2000 feet high, cascades coming over them,
and the river flowing through the meadows and groves
of the level bottom in tranquil, richly-embowered
reaches.

Beyond this Little Yosemite in the main canyon,
there are three other little yosemites, the highest situated a few miles below the base of Mount Lyell, at
an elevation of about 7800 feet above the sea. To describe these, with all their wealth of Yosemite furni-
ture, and the wilderness of lofty peaks above them, the
home of the avalanche and treasury of the fountain

snow, would take us far beyond the bounds of a single book. Nor can we here consider the formation of these mountain landscapes—how the crystal rocks were brought to light by glaciers made up of crystal snow, making beauty whose influence is so mysterious on everyone who sees it.

Of the small glacier lakes so characteristic of these upper regions, there are no fewer than sixty-seven in the basin of the main middle branch, besides countless smaller pools. In the basin of the Illilouette there are sixteen, in the Tenaya basin and its branches thirteen, in the Yosemite Creek basin fourteen, and in the Pohono or Bridal Veil one, making a grand total of one hundred and eleven lakes whose waters come to sing at Yosemite. So glorious is the background of the great Valley, so harmonious its relations to its widespreading fountains.

The same harmony prevails in all the other features of the adjacent landscapes. Climbing out of the Valley by the subordinate canyons, we find the ground rising from the brink of the walls: on the south side to the fountains of the Bridal Veil Creek, the basin of which is noted for the beauty of its meadows and its superb forests of silver fir; on the north side through the basin of the Yosemite Creek to the dividing ridge along the Tuolumne Canyon and the fountains of the Hoffman Range.

DOWN THE YOSEMITE CREEK

In general views the Yosemite Creek basin seems to be paved with domes and smooth, whaleback masses of granite in every stage of development—some showing only their crowns; others rising high and free above the girdling forests, singly or in groups. Others are developed only on one side, forming bold outstanding bosses usually well fringed with shrubs and trees, and presenting the polished surfaces given them by the glacier that brought them into relief. On the upper portion of the basin broad moraine beds have been deposited and on these fine, thrifty forests are growing. Lakes and meadows and small spongy bogs may be found hiding here and there in the woods or back in the fountain recesses of Mount Hoffman, while a thousand gardens are planted along the banks of the streams.

All the wide, fan-shaped upper portion of the basin is covered with a network of small rills that go cheerily on their way to their grand fall in the Valley, now flowing on smooth pavements in sheets thin as glass, now diving under willows and laving their red roots, oozing through green, plushy bogs, plashing over small falls and dancing down slanting cascades, calming again, gliding through patches of smooth glacier meadows with sod of alpine agrostis mixed with blue and white violets and daisies, breaking, tossing among rough boulders and fallen trees, resting in calm pools, flowing together until, all united, they go to their fate with stately, tranquil gestures like a full-grown river. At the crossing of the Mono Trail, about two miles above the head of the Yosemite Fall, the stream is nearly forty feet wide, and when the snow is melting rapidly in the spring it is about four feet deep, with a current of two and a half miles an hour. This is about the volume of water that forms the Fall in May and June when there had been much snow the preceding winter; but it varies greatly from month to month. The snow rapidly vanishes from the open portion of the basin, which faces southward, and only a few of the tributaries reach back to perennial snow and ice fountains in the shadowy amphitheaters on the precipitous northern slopes of Mount Hoffman. The total descent made by the stream from its highest sources to its confluence with the Merced in the Valley is about 6000 feet, while the distance is only about ten miles, an average fall of 600 feet per mile. The last mile of its course lies between the sides of sunken domes and swelling folds of the granite that are clustered and pressed together like a mass of bossy cumulus clouds. Through this shining way Yosemite Creek goes to its fate, swaying and swirling with easy, graceful gestures and singing the last of its mountain songs before it reaches the dizzy edge of Yosemite to fall 2600 feet into another world, where climate, vegetation, inhabitants, all are different. Emerging from this last canyon the stream glides, in flat, lace-like folds, down a smooth incline into a small pool where it seems to rest and compose itself before taking the grand plunge. Then calmly, as if leaving a lake, it slips over the polished lip of the pool down another incline and out over the brow of the precipice in a magnificent curve thick-sown with rainbow spray.

THE YOSEMITE FALL

Long ago before I had traced this fine stream to its head back of Mount Hoffman, I was eager to reach the extreme verge to see how it behaved in flying so far through the air; but after enjoying this view and getting safely away I have never advised anyone to follow my steps. The last incline down which the stream journeys so gracefully is so steep and smooth one must slip cautiously forward on hands and feet alongside the rushing water, which so near one's head is very exciting. But to gain a perfect view one must go yet farther, over a curving brow to a slight shelf on the extreme brink. This shelf, formed by the flaking off of a fold of granite, is about three inches wide, just wide enough for a safe rest for one's heels. To me it seemed nerve-trying to slip to this narrow foothold and poise on the

edge of such a precipice so close to the confusing whirl
of the waters; and after casting longing glances over
the shining brow of the fall and listening to its sublime
psalm, I concluded not to attempt to go nearer, but,
nevertheless, against reasonable judgment, I did. No-
ticing some tufts of artemisia in a cleft of rock, I filled
my mouth with the leaves, hoping their bitter taste
might help to keep caution keen and prevent giddi-
ness. In spite of myself I reached the little ledge, got
my heels well set, and worked sidewise twenty or
thirty feet to a point close to the out-plunging current.
Here the view is perfectly free down into the heart of
the bright irised throng of comet-like streamers into
which the whole ponderous volume of the fall sepa-
rates, two or three hundred feet below the brow. So
glorious a display of pure wildness, acting at close
range while cut off from all the world beside, is terribly impressive. A less nerve-trying view may be obtained from a fissured portion of the edge of the cliff
about forty yards to the eastward of the fall. Seen from
this point towards noon, in the spring, the rainbow on
its brow seems to be broken up and mingled with the
rushing comets until all the fall is stained with iris
colors, leaving no white water visible. This is the best
of the safe views from above, the huge steadfast rocks,
the flying waters, and the rainbow light forming one
of the most glorious pictures conceivable.

The Yosemite Fall is separated into an upper and a
lower fall with a series of falls and cascades between
them, but when viewed in front from the bottom of
the Valley they all appear as one.

So grandly does this magnificent fall display itself
from the floor of the Valley, few visitors take the
trouble to climb the walls to gain nearer views, unable
to realize how vastly more impressive it is near by than
at a distance of one or two miles.

A WONDERFUL ASCENT

The views developed in a walk up the zigzags of the trail leading to the foot of the Upper Fall are about as varied and impressive as those displayed along the favorite Glacier Point Trail. One rises as if on wings. The groves, meadows, fern-flats and reaches of the river gain new interest, as if never seen before; all the views changing in a most striking manner as we go higher from point to point. The foreground also changes every few rods in the most surprising manner, although the earthquake talus and the level bench on the face of the wall over which the trail passes seem monotonous and commonplace as seen from the bottom of the Valley. Up we climb with glad exhilaration, through shaggy fringes of laurel, ceanothus, glossy-leaved manzanita and live-oak, from shadow to shadow across bars and patches of sunshine, the leafy openings making charming frames for the Valley pictures beheld through them, and for the glimpses of the high peaks that appear in the distance. The higher we go the farther we seem to be from the summit of the vast granite wall. Here we pass a projecting buttress whose grooved and rounded surface tells a plain story of the time when the Valley, now filled with sunshine, was filled with ice, when the grand old Yosemite Glacier, flowing river-like from its distant fountains, swept through it, crushing, grinding, wearing its way ever deeper, developing and fashioning these sublime rocks. Again we cross a white, battered gully, the pathway of rock avalanches or snow avalanches. Farther on we come to a gentle stream slipping down the face of the cliff in lace-like strips, and dropping from ledge to ledge—too small to be called a fall—trickling, dripping, oozing, a pathless wanderer from one of the upland meadows lying a little way

back of the Valley rim, seeking a way century after
century to the depths of the Valley without any appreciable channel. Every morning after a cool night,
evaporation being checked, it gathers strength and
sings like a bird, but as the day advances and the sun
strikes its thin currents outspread on the heated precipices, most of its waters vanish ere the bottom of the
Valley is reached. Many a fine, hanging-garden aloft
on breezy inaccessible heights owes to it its freshness
and fullness of beauty; ferneries in shady nooks, filled
with adiantum, woodwardia, woodsia, aspidium,[6]
pellaea, and cheilanthes, rosetted and tufted and
ranged in lines, daintily overlapping, thatching the
stupendous cliffs with softest beauty, some of the delicate fronds seeming to float on the warm moist air,
without any connection with rock or stream. Nor is
there any lack of colored plants wherever they can
find a place to cling to; lilies and mints, the showy
cardinal mimulus, and glowing cushions of the golden
bahia,[7] enlivened with butterflies and bees and all the
other small, happy humming creatures that belong to
them.

After the highest point on the lower division of the
trail is gained it leads up into the deep recess occupied
by the great fall, the noblest display of falling water
to be found in the Valley, or perhaps in the world.
When it first comes in sight it seems almost within
reach of one's hand, so great in the spring is its volume
and velocity, yet it is still nearly a third of a mile
away and appears to recede as we advance. The
sculpture of the walls about it is on a scale of grandeur,
according nobly with the fall—plain and massive,
though elaborately finished, like all the other cliffs
about the Valley.

6 *Dryopteris*.
7 An *Eriophyllum*.

In the afternoon an immense shadow is cast athwart the plateau in front of the fall, and over the chaparral bushes that clothe the slopes and benches of the walls to the eastward, creeping upward until the fall is wholly overcast, the contrast between the shaded and illumined sections being very striking in these near views.

Under this shadow, during the cool centuries immediately following the breaking-up of the Glacial Period, dwelt a small residual glacier, one of the few that lingered on this sun-beaten side of the Valley after the main trunk glacier had vanished. It sent down a long winding current through the narrow canyon on the west side of the fall, and must have formed a striking feature of the ancient scenery of the Valley; the lofty fall of ice and fall of water side by side, yet separate and distinct.

The coolness of the afternoon shadow and the abundant dewy spray make a fine climate for the plateau ferns and grasses, and for the beautiful azalea bushes that grow here in profusion and bloom in September, long after the warmer thickets down on the floor of the Valley have withered and gone to seed. Even close to the fall, and behind it at the base of the cliff, a few venturesome plants may be found undisturbed by the rock-shaking torrent.

The basin at the foot of the fall into which the current directly pours, when it is not swayed by the wind, is about ten feet deep and fifteen to twenty feet in diameter. That it is not much deeper is surprising, when the great height and force of the fall is considered. But the rock where the water strikes probably suffers less erosion than it would were the descent less than half as great, since the current is outspread, and much of its force is spent ere it reaches the bottom— being received on the air as upon an elastic cushion, and borne outward and dissipated over a surface more than fifty yards wide.

This surface, easily examined when the water is low, is intensely clean and fresh-looking. It is the raw, quick flesh of the mountain wholly untouched by the weather. In summer droughts, when the snowfall of the preceding winter has been light, the fall is reduced to a mere shower of separate drops without any obscuring spray. Then we may safely go back of it and view the crystal shower from beneath, each drop wavering and pulsing as it makes its way through the air, and flashing off jets of colored light of ravishing beauty. But all this is invisible from the bottom of the Valley, like a thousand other interesting things. One must labor for beauty as for bread, here as elsewhere.

THE GRANDEUR OF THE YOSEMITE FALL

During the time of the spring floods the best near view of the fall is obtained from Fern Ledge on the east side above the blinding spray at a height of about 400 feet above the base of the fall. A climb of about 1400 feet from the Valley has to be made, and there is no trail, but to anyone fond of climbing this will make the ascent all the more delightful. A narrow part of the ledge extends to the side of the fall and back of it, enabling us to approach it as closely as we wish. When the afternoon sunshine is streaming through the throng of comets, ever wasting, ever renewed, the marvelous fineness, firmness and variety of their forms are beautifully revealed. At the top of the fall they seem to burst forth in irregular spurts from some grand, throbbing mountain heart. Now and then one mighty throb sends forth a mass of solid water into the free air far beyond the others, which rushes alone to the bottom of the fall with long streaming tail, like combed silk, while the others, descending in clusters, gradually mingle and lose their identity. But they all rush past us with amazing velocity and display of power, though apparently drowsy and deliberate in their movements when observed from a distance of a mile or two. The heads of these comet-like masses are composed of nearly solid water, and are dense white in color like pressed snow, from the friction they suffer in rushing through the air, the portion worn off forming the tail, between the white lustrous threads and films of which faint, grayish pencilings appear, while the outer, finer sprays of water-dust, whirling in sunny eddies, are pearly gray throughout. At the bottom of the fall there is but little distinction of form visible. It is mostly a hissing, clashing, seething, upwhirling mass of scud and spray, through which the light sifts in gray and purple tones, while at times when the sun strikes at the required angle, the whole wild and apparently lawless, stormy, striving mass is changed to brilliant rainbow hues, manifesting finest harmony. The middle portion of the fall is the most openly beautiful; lower, the various forms into which the waters are wrought are more closely and voluminously veiled, while higher, towards the head, the current is comparatively simple and undivided. But even at the bottom, in the boiling clouds of spray, there is no confusion, while the rainbow light makes all divine, adding glorious beauty and peace to glorious power. This noble fall has far the richest, as well as the most powerful, voice of all the falls of the Valley, its tones varying from the sharp hiss and rustle of the wind in the glossy leaves of the live-oaks and the soft, sifting, hushing tones of the pines, to the loudest rush and roar of storm winds and thunder among the crags of the summit peaks. The low bass, booming, reverberating tones, heard under favorable circumstances five or six miles away, are formed by the dashing and ex-

ploding of heavy masses mixed with air upon two
projecting ledges on the face of the cliff, the one on
which we are standing and another about 200 feet
above it. The torrent of massive comets is continuous
at time of high water, while the explosive, booming
notes are wildly intermittent, because, unless influenced by the wind, most of the heavier masses shoot
out from the face of the precipice, and pass the ledges
upon which at other times they are exploded. Occasionally the whole fall is swayed away from the front
of the cliff, then suddenly dashed flat against it, or
vibrated from side to side like a pendulum, giving rise
to endless variety of forms and sounds.

THE NEVADA FALL

The Nevada Fall is 600 feet high and is usually
ranked next to the Yosemite in general interest among
the five main falls of the Valley. Coming through the
Little Yosemite in tranquil reaches, the river is first
broken into rapids on a moraine boulder-bar that
crosses the lower end of the valley. Thence it pursues
its way to the head of the fall in a rough, solid rock
channel, dashing on side angles, heaving in heavy
surging masses against elbow knobs, and swirling and
swashing in potholes without a moment's rest. Thus,
already chafed and dashed to foam, overfolded and
twisted, it plunges over the brink of the precipice as if
glad to escape into the open air. But before it reaches
the bottom it is pulverized yet finer by impinging upon
a sloping portion of the cliff about half-way down, thus
making it the whitest of all the falls of the Valley, and
altogether one of the most wonderful in the world.

On the north side, close to its head, a slab of granite
projects over the brink, forming a fine point for a view,
over its throng of streamers and wild plunging, into its
intensely white bosom, and, through the broad drifts

of spray, to the river far below, gathering its spent waters and rushing on again down the canyon in glad exultation into Emerald Pool, where at length it grows calm and gets rest for what still lies before it. All the features of the view correspond with the waters in grandeur and wildness. The glacier-sculptured walls of the canyon on either hand, with the sublime mass of the Glacier Point Ridge in front, form a huge triangular pit-like basin, which, filled with the roaring of the falling river, seems as if it might be the hopper of one of the mills of the gods in which the mountains were being ground.

THE VERNAL FALL

The Vernal, about a mile below the Nevada, is 400 feet high, a staid, orderly, graceful, easy-going fall, proper and exact in every movement and gesture, with scarce a hint of the passionate enthusiasm of the Yosemite or of the impetuous Nevada, whose chafed and twisted waters hurrying over the cliff seem glad to escape into the open air, while its deep, booming, thunder-tones reverberate over the listening landscape. Nevertheless it is a favorite with most visitors, doubtless because it is more accessible than any other, more closely approached and better seen and heard. A good stairway ascends the cliff beside it[8] and the level plateau at the head enables one to saunter safely along the edge of the river as it comes from Emerald Pool and to watch its waters, calmly bending over the brow of the precipice, in a sheet eighty feet wide, changing in color from green to purplish gray and white until dashed on a boulder talus. Thence issuing from beneath its fine broad spray-clouds we see the tremendously adventurous river still unspent, beating

[8] Mist Trail.

its way down the wildest and deepest of all its canyons in gray roaring rapids, dear to the ouzel, and below the confluence of the Illilouette, sweeping around the shoulder of the Half Dome on its approach to the head of the tranquil levels of the Valley.

THE ILLILOUETTE FALL

The Illilouette in general appearance most resembles the Nevada. The volume of water is less than half as great, but it is about the same height (600 feet) and its waters receive the same kind of preliminary tossing in a rocky, irregular channel. Therefore it is a very white and fine-grained fall. When it is in full springtime bloom it is partly divided by rocks that roughen the lip of the precipice, but this division amounts only to a kind of fluting and grooving of the column, which has a beautiful effect. It is not nearly so grand a fall as the upper Yosemite, or so symmetrical as the Vernal, or so airily graceful and simple as the Bridal Veil, nor does it ever display so tremendous an outgush of snowy magnificence as the Nevada; but in the exquisite fineness and richness of texture of its flowing folds it surpasses them all.

One of the finest effects of sunlight on falling water I ever saw in Yosemite or elsewhere I found on the brow of this beautiful fall. It was in the Indian summer, when the leaf colors were ripe and the great cliffs and domes were transfigured in the hazy golden air. I had scrambled up its rugged talus-dammed canyon, oftentimes stopping to take breath and look back to admire the wonderful views to be had there of the great Half Dome, and to enjoy the extreme purity of the water, which in the motionless pools on this stream is almost perfectly invisible; the colored foliage of the maples, dogwoods, *Rubus* tangles, etc., and the late goldenrods and asters. The voice of the fall was now low, and the grand spring and summer floods had waned to sifting, drifting gauze and thin-broidered folds of linked and arrowy lace-work. When I reached the foot of the fall sunbeams were glinting across its head, leaving all the rest of it in shadow; and on its illumined brow a group of yellow spangles of singular form and beauty were playing, flashing up and dancing in large flame-shaped masses, wavering at times, then steadying, rising and falling in accord with the shifting forms of the water. But the color of the dancing spangles changed not at all. Nothing in clouds or flowers, on bird-wings or the lips of shells, could rival it in fineness. It was the most divinely beautiful mass of rejoicing yellow light I ever beheld—one of Nature's precious gifts that perchance may come to us but once in a lifetime.

THE MINOR FALLS

There are many other comparatively small falls and cascades in the Valley. The most notable are the Yosemite Gorge Fall and Cascades, Tenaya Fall and Cascades, Royal Arch Falls, the two Sentinel Cascades and the falls of Cascade and Tamarack Creeks, a mile or two below the lower end of the Valley. These last are often visited. The others are seldom noticed or mentioned; although in almost any other country they would be visited and described as wonders.

The six intermediate falls in the gorge between the head of the Lower and the base of the Upper Yosemite Falls, separated by a few deep pools and strips of rapids, and three slender, tributary cascades on the west side form a series more strikingly varied and combined than any other in the Valley, yet very few of all the Valley visitors ever see them or hear of them. No available standpoint commands a view of them all. The best general view is obtained from the mouth of

the gorge near the head of the Lower Fall. The two
lowest of the series, together with one of the three
tributary cascades, are visible from this standpoint, but
in reaching it the last twenty or thirty feet of the
descent is rather dangerous in time of high water, the
shelving rocks being then slippery on account of spray,
but if one should chance to slip when the water is low,
only a bump or two and a harmless plash would be the
penalty. No part of the gorge, however, is safe to any
but cautious climbers.

Though the dark gorge hall of these rejoicing waters
is never flushed by the purple light of morning or evening, it is warmed and cheered by the white light of
noonday, which, falling into so much foam and spray
of varying degrees of fineness, makes marvelous displays of rainbow colors. So filled, indeed, is it with
this precious light, at favorable times it seems to take
the place of common air. Laurel bushes shed fragrance
into it from above and live-oaks, those fearless mountaineers, hold fast to angular seams and lean out over
it with their fringing sprays and bright mirror leaves.

One bird, the ouzel, loves this gorge and flies
through it merrily, or cheerily, rather, stopping to sing
on foam-washed bosses where other birds could find
no rest for their feet. I have even seen a gray squirrel
down in the heart of it beside the wild rejoicing water.

One of my favorite night walks was along the rim of
this wild gorge in times of high water when the moon
was full, to see the lunar bows in the spray.

For about a mile above Mirror Lake the Tenaya
Canyon is level, and richly planted with fir, Douglas
spruce and libocedrus, forming a remarkably fine
grove, at the head of which is the Tenaya Fall. Though
seldom seen or described, this is, I think, the most
picturesque of all the small falls. A considerable distance above it, Tenaya Creek comes hurrying down,

white and foamy, over a flat pavement inclined at an angle of about eighteen degrees. In time of high water this sheet of rapids is nearly seventy feet wide, and is varied in a very striking way by three parallel furrows that extend in the direction of its flow. These furrows, worn by the action of the stream upon cleavage joints, vary in width, are slightly sinuous, and have large boulders firmly wedged in them here and there in narrow places, giving rise, of course, to a complicated series of wild dashes, doublings, and upleaping arches in the swift torrent. Just before it reaches the head of the fall the current is divided, the left division making a vertical drop of about eighty feet in a romantic, leafy, flowery, mossy nook, while the other forms a rugged cascade.

The Royal Arch Fall in time of high water is a magnificent object, forming a broad ornamental sheet in front of the arches. The two Sentinel Cascades, 3000 feet high, are also grand spectacles when the snow is melting fast in the spring, but by the middle of summer they have diminished to mere streaks scarce noticeable amid their sublime surroundings.

THE BEAUTY OF THE RAINBOWS

The Bridal Veil and Vernal Falls are famous for their rainbows; and special visits to them are often made when the sun shines into the spray at the most favorable angle. But amid the spray and foam and fine-ground mist ever rising from the various falls and cataracts there is an affluence and variety of iris bows scarcely known to visitors who stay only a day or two. Both day and night, winter and summer, this divine light may be seen wherever water is falling, dancing, singing; telling the heart-peace of Nature amid the wildest displays of her power. In the bright spring mornings the black-walled recess at the foot of the

Lower Yosemite Fall is lavishly filled with irised spray;
and not simply does this span the dashing foam, but
the foam itself, the whole mass of it, beheld at a certain distance, seems to be colored, and drifts and wa-
vers from color to color, mingling with the foliage of
the adjacent trees, without suggesting any relationship
to the ordinary rainbow. This is perhaps the largest
and most reservoir-like fountain of iris colors to be
found in the Valley.

Lunar rainbows or spray-bows also abound in the
glorious affluence of dashing, rejoicing, hurrahing, enthusiastic spring floods, their colors as distinct as those
of the sun and regularly and obviously banded, though
less vivid. Fine specimens may be found any night
at the foot of the Upper Yosemite Fall, glowing gloriously amid the gloomy shadows and thundering waters, whenever there is plenty of moonlight and spray.
Even the secondary bow is at times distinctly visible.

The best point from which to observe them is on
Fern Ledge. For some time after moonrise, at time of
high water, the arc has a span of about five hundred
feet, and is set upright; one end planted in the boiling spray at the bottom, the other in the edge of the
fall, creeping lower, of course, and becoming less upright as the moon rises higher. This grand arc of color,
glowing in mild, shapely beauty in so weird and huge
a chamber of night shadows, and amid the rush and
roar and tumultuous dashing of this thunder-voiced
fall, is one of the most impressive and most cheering
of all the blessed mountain evangels.

Smaller bows may be seen in the gorge on the plateau between the Upper and Lower Falls. Once toward midnight, after spending a few hours with the
wild beauty of the Upper Fall, I sauntered along the
edge of the gorge, looking in here and there, wherever
the footing felt safe, to see what I could learn of the

night aspects of the smaller falls that dwell there. And down in an exceedingly black, pit-like portion of the gorge, at the foot of the highest of the intermediate falls, into which the moonbeams were pouring through a narrow opening, I saw a well-defined spray-bow, beautifully distinct in colors, spanning the pit from side to side, while pure white foam-waves beneath the beautiful bow were constantly springing up out of the dark into the moonlight like dancing ghosts.

AN UNEXPECTED ADVENTURE

A wild scene, but not a safe one, is made by the moon as it appears through the edge of the Yosemite Fall when one is behind it. Once, after enjoying the night-song of the waters and watching the formation of the colored bow as the moon came round the domes and sent her beams into the wild uproar, I ventured out on the narrow bench that extends back of the fall from Fern Ledge and began to admire the dim-veiled grandeur of the view. I could see the fine gauzy threads of the fall's filmy border by having the light in front; and wishing to look at the moon through the meshes of some of the denser portions of the fall, I ventured to creep farther behind it while it was gently wind-swayed, without taking sufficient thought about the consequences of its swaying back to its natural position after the wind-pressure should be removed. The effect was enchanting: fine, savage music sounding above, beneath, around me; while the moon, apparently in the very midst of the rushing waters, seemed to be struggling to keep her place, on account of the ever-varying form and density of the water masses through which she was seen, now darkly veiled or eclipsed by a rush of thick-headed comets, now flashing out through openings between their tails. I was in fairyland between the dark wall and the wild throng

of illumined waters, but suffered sudden disenchant-
ment; for, like the witch-scene in Alloway Kirk, "in
an instant all was dark." Down came a dash of spent
comets, thin and harmless-looking in the distance, but
they felt desperately solid and stony when they struck
my shoulders, like a mixture of choking spray and
gravel and big hailstones. Instinctively dropping on
my knees, I gripped an angle of the rock, curled up
like a young fern frond with my face pressed against
my breast, and in this attitude submitted as best I
could to my thundering bath. The heavier masses
seemed to strike like cobblestones, and there was a
confused noise of many waters about my ears—hissing, gurgling, clashing sounds that were not heard as
music. The situation was quickly realized. How fast
one's thoughts burn in such times of stress! I was
weighing chances of escape. Would the column be
swayed a few inches away from the wall, or would it
come yet closer? The fall was in flood and not so
lightly would its ponderous mass be swayed. My fate
seemed to depend on a breath of the "idle wind." It
was moved gently forward, the pounding ceased, and
I was once more visited by glimpses of the moon. But
fearing I might be caught at a disadvantage in making
too hasty a retreat, I moved only a few feet along the
bench to where a block of ice lay. I wedged myself
between the ice and the wall, and lay face down-
wards, until the steadiness of the light gave encourage-
ment to rise and get away. Somewhat nerve-shaken,
drenched, and benumbed, I made out to build a fire,
warmed myself, ran home, reached my cabin[9] before
daylight, got an hour or two of sleep, and awoke

[9] Presumably his first Yosemite cabin, "a little shanty made
of sugar pine shingles" which he built in 1869 and occupied
until January, 1871. It was located on Yosemite Creek near the
foot of the Lower Fall.

sound and comfortable, better, not worse, for my hard midnight bath.

CLIMATE AND WEATHER

Owing to the westerly trend of the Valley and its vast depth there is a great difference between the climates of the north and south sides—greater than between many countries far apart; for the south wall is in shadow during the winter months, while the north is bathed in sunshine every clear day. Thus there is mild spring weather on one side of the Valley while winter rules the other. Far up the north-side cliffs many a nook may be found closely embraced by sun-beaten rock-bosses in which flowers bloom every month of the year. Even butterflies may be seen in these high winter gardens except when snow-storms are falling and a few days after they have ceased. Near the head of the lower Yosemite Fall in January I found the ant lions lying in wait in their warm sand-cups, rock ferns being unrolled, club mosses covered with fresh-growing points, the flowers of the laurel nearly open, and the honeysuckle rosetted with bright young leaves; every plant seemed to be thinking about summer. Even on the shadow-side of the Valley the frost is never very sharp. The lowest temperature I ever observed during four winters was 7° Fahrenheit. The first twenty-four days of January had an average temperature at 9 A.M. of 32°, minimum 22°; at 3 P.M. the average was 40° 30', the minimum 32°. Along the top of the walls, 7000 and 8000 feet high, the temperature was, of course, much lower. But the difference in temperature between the north and south sides is due not so much to the winter sunshine as to the heat of the preceding summer, stored up in the rocks, which rapidly melts the snow in contact with them. For though summer sun-heat is stored in the rocks of the south side also, the amount is much less because the rays fall obliquely on the south wall even in summer and almost vertically on the north.

The upper branches of the Yosemite streams are buried every winter beneath a heavy mantle of snow, and set free in the spring in magnificent floods. Then, all the fountains, full and overflowing, every living thing breaks forth into singing, and the glad exulting streams, shining and falling in the warm sunny weather, shake everything into music, making all the mountain-world a song.

The great annual spring thaw usually begins in May in the forest region, and in June and July on the high Sierra, varying somewhat both in time and fullness with the weather and the depth of the snow. Toward the end of summer the streams are at their lowest ebb, few even of the strongest singing much above a whisper as they slip and ripple through gravel and boulder-beds from pool to pool in the hollows of their channels, and drop in pattering showers like rain, and slip down precipices and fall in sheets of embroidery, fold over fold. But, however low their singing, it is always ineffably fine in tone, in harmony with the restful time of the year.

The first snow of the season that comes to the help of the streams usually falls in September or October, sometimes even in the latter part of August, in the midst of yellow Indian summer, when the goldenrods and gentians of the glacier meadows are in their prime. This Indian-summer snow, however, soon melts, the chilled flowers spread their petals to the sun, and the gardens as well as the streams are refreshed as if only a warm shower had fallen. The snowstorms that load the mountains to form the main fountain supply for the year seldom set in before the middle or end of November.

WINTER BEAUTY OF THE VALLEY

When the first heavy storms stopped work on the high mountains, I made haste down to my Yosemite den, not to "hole up" and sleep the white months away; I was out every day, and often all night, sleeping but little, studying the so-called wonders and common things ever on show, wading, climbing, sauntering among the blessed storms and calms, rejoicing in almost everything alike that I could see or hear: the glorious brightness of frosty mornings; the sunbeams pouring over the white domes and crags into the groves and waterfalls, kindling marvelous iris fires in the hoarfrost and spray; the great forests and mountains in their deep noon sleep; the good-night alpenglow; the stars; the solemn gazing moon, drawing the huge domes and headlands one by one glowing white out of the shadows hushed and breathless like an audience in awful enthusiasm, while the meadows at their feet sparkle with frost-stars like the sky; the sublime darkness of storm-nights, when all the lights are out; the clouds in whose depths the frail snow-flowers grow; the behavior and many voices of the different kinds of storms, trees, birds, waterfalls, and snow-avalanches in the ever-changing weather.

Every clear, frosty morning loud sounds are heard booming and reverberating from side to side of the Valley at intervals of a few minutes, beginning soon after sunrise and continuing an hour or two like a thunder-storm. In my first winter in the Valley I could not make out the source of this noise. I thought of falling boulders, rock-blasting, etc. Not till I saw what looked like hoarfrost dropping from the side of the Fall was the problem explained. The strange thunder is made by the fall of sections of ice formed of spray that is frozen on the face of the cliff along the sides of the

Upper Yosemite Fall—a sort of crystal plaster, a foot
or two thick, cracked off by the sunbeams, awakening
all the Valley like cock-crowing, announcing the finest
weather, shouting aloud Nature's infinite industry and
love of hard work in creating beauty.

EXPLORING AN ICE CONE

This frozen spray gives rise to one of the most interesting winter features of the Valley—a cone of ice
at the foot of the fall, four or five hundred feet high.
From the Fern Ledge standpoint its crater-like throat
is seen, down which the fall plunges with deep, gasp-
ing explosions of compressed air, and, after being well
churned in the stormy interior, the water bursts forth
through arched openings at its base, apparently
scourged and weary and glad to escape, while belch-
ing spray, spouted up out of the throat past the descending current, is wafted away in irised drifts to the
adjacent rocks and groves. It is built during the night
and early hours of the morning; only in spells of ex-
ceptionally cold and cloudy weather is the work continued through the day. The greater part of the spray
material falls in crystalline showers direct to its place,
something like a small local snowstorm; but a considerable portion is first frozen on the face of the cliff
along the sides of the fall and stays there until ex-
panded and cracked off in irregular masses, some of
them tons in weight, to be built into the walls of the
cone; while in windy, frosty weather, when the fall is
swayed from side to side, the cone is well drenched
and the loose ice masses and spray-dust are all firmly
welded and frozen together. Thus the finest of the
downy wafts and curls of spray-dust, which in mild
nights fall about as silently as dew, are held back until
sunrise to make a store of heavy ice to reinforce the
waterfall's thunder-tones.

While the cone is in process of formation, growing higher and wider in the frosty weather, it looks like a beautiful smooth, pure-white hill; but when it is wasting and breaking up in the spring its surface is strewn with leaves, pine branches, stones, sand, etc., that have been brought over the fall, making it look like a heap of avalanche detritus.

Anxious to learn what I could about the structure of this curious hill I often approached it in calm weather and tried to climb it, carrying an ax to cut steps. Once I nearly succeeded in gaining the summit. At the base I was met by a current of spray and wind that made seeing and breathing difficult. I pushed on backward, however, and soon gained the slope of the hill, where by creeping close to the surface most of the choking blast passed over me and I managed to crawl up with but little difficulty. Thus I made my way nearly to the summit, halting at times to peer up through the wild whirls of spray at the veiled grandeur of the fall, or to listen to the thunder beneath me; the whole hill was sounding as if it were a huge, bellowing drum. I hoped that by waiting until the fall was blown aslant I should be able to climb to the lip of the crater and get a view of the interior; but a suffocating blast, half air, half water, followed by the fall of an enormous mass of frozen spray from a spot high up on the wall, quickly discouraged me. The whole cone was jarred by the blow and some fragments of the mass sped past me dangerously near; so I beat a hasty retreat, chilled and drenched, and lay down on a sunny rock to dry.

Once during a wind-storm when I saw that the fall was frequently blown westward, leaving the cone dry, I ran up to Fern Ledge hoping to gain a clear view of the interior. I set out at noon. All the way up the storm notes were so loud about me that the voice of the fall

was almost drowned by them. Notwithstanding the
rocks and bushes everywhere were drenched by the
wind-driven spray, I approached the brink of the precipice overlooking the mouth of the ice cone, but I was
almost suffocated by the drenching, gusty spray, and
was compelled to seek shelter. I searched for some
hiding-place in the wall from whence I might run out
at some opportune moment when the fall with its
whirling spray and torn shreds of comet tails and trailing, tattered skirts was borne westward, as I had seen
it carried several times before, leaving the cliffs on
the east side and the ice hill bare in the sunlight. I
had not long to wait, for, as if ordered so for my special accommodation, the mighty downrush of comets
with their whirling drapery swung westward and remained aslant for nearly half an hour. The cone was
admirably lighted and deserted by the water, which
fell most of the time on the rocky western slopes
mostly outside of the cone. The mouth into which the
fall pours was, as near as I could guess, about one hundred feet in diameter north and south and about two
hundred feet east and west, which is about the shape
and size of the fall at its best in its normal condition
at this season.

The crater-like opening was not a true oval, but
more like a huge coarse mouth. I could see down the
throat about one hundred feet or perhaps farther.[10]

The fall precipice overhangs from a height of 400

[10] Park naturalists observe that the ice cone at the base of
Upper Yosemite Fall usually reaches its maximum size by late
March. It is generally 200 to 250 feet high. A survey in 1937
resulted in calculations that a cone photographed during Muir's
lifetime was one of the largest ever recorded. Estimates were
that the height of the cone was 322 feet, and that it contained
a volume of 25 million cubic feet of ice and snow. Smaller ice
cones are formed at the bases of the other waterfalls in the
Valley.

feet above the base; therefore the water strikes some distance from the base of the cliff, allowing space for the accumulation of a considerable mass of ice between the fall and the wall.

II
WINTER STORMS AND SPRING FLOODS

The Bridal Veil and the Upper Yosemite Falls, on account of their height and exposure, are greatly influenced by winds. The common summer winds that come up the river canyon from the plains are seldom very strong; but the north winds do some very wild work, worrying the falls and the forests, and hanging snow-banners on the comet-peaks. One wild winter morning I was awakened by a storm-wind that was playing with the falls as if they were mere wisps of mist and making the great pines bow and sing with glorious enthusiasm. The Valley had been visited a short time before by a series of fine snowstorms, and the floor and the cliffs and all the region round about were lavishly adorned with its best winter jewelry, the air was full of fine snow-dust, and pine branches, tassels and empty cones were flying in an almost continuous flock.

Soon after sunrise, when I was seeking a place safe from flying branches, I saw the Lower Yosemite Fall thrashed and pulverized from top to bottom into one glorious mass of rainbow dust; while a thousand feet above it the main Upper Fall was suspended on the face of the cliff in the form of an inverted bow, all silvery white and fringed with short wavering strips. Then, suddenly assailed by a tremendous blast, the whole mass of the fall was blown into threads and ribbons, and driven back over the brow of the cliff whence it came, as if denied admission to the Valley. This kind of storm-work was continued about ten or fifteen minutes; then another change in the play of the huge exulting swirls and billows and upheaving domes of the gale allowed the baffled fall to gather and arrange its tattered waters, and sink down again in its place. As the day advanced, the gale gave no sign of dying, excepting brief lulls, the Valley was filled with its weariless roar, and the cloudless sky grew garish-white from myriads of minute, sparkling snow-spicules. In the afternoon, while I watched the Upper Fall from the shelter of a big pine tree, it was suddenly arrested in its descent at a point about half-way down, and was neither blown upward nor driven aside, but simply held stationary in mid-air, as if gravitation below that point in the path of its descent had ceased to act. The ponderous flood, weighing hundreds of tons, was sustained, hovering, hesitating, like a bunch of thistledown, while I counted one hundred and ninety. All this time the ordinary amount of water was coming over the cliff and accumulating in the air, swedging and widening and forming an irregular cone about seven hundred feet high, tapering to the top of the wall, the whole standing still, resting on the invisible arm of the North Wind. At length, as if commanded to go on again, scores of arrowy comets shot forth from the bottom of the suspended mass as if escaping from separate outlets.

The brow of El Capitan was decked with long snow-streamers like hair, Clouds Rest was fairly enveloped in drifting gossamer films, and the Half Dome loomed up in the garish light like a majestic, living creature clad in the same gauzy, wind-woven drapery, while upward currents meeting at times overhead made it smoke like a volcano.

AN EXTRAORDINARY STORM AND FLOOD

Glorious as are these rocks and waters arrayed in storm robes, or chanting rejoicing in every-day dress, they are still more glorious when rare weather conditions meet to make them sing with floods. Only once during all the years I have lived in the Valley have I seen it in full flood bloom. In 1871 the early winter weather was delightful; the days all sunshine, the nights all starry and calm, calling forth fine crops of frost-crystals on the pines and withered ferns and grasses for the morning sunbeams to sift through. In the afternoon of December 16, when I was sauntering on the meadows, I noticed a massive crimson cloud growing in solitary grandeur above the Cathedral Rocks, its form scarcely less striking than its color. It had a picturesque, bulging base like an old sequoia, a smooth, tapering stem, and a bossy, down-curling crown like a mushroom; all its parts were colored alike, making one mass of translucent crimson. Wondering what the meaning of that strange, lonely red cloud might be, I was up betimes next morning looking at the weather, but all seemed tranquil as yet. Towards noon gray clouds with a close, curly grain like bird's-eye maple began to grow, and late at night rain fell, which soon changed to snow. Next morning the snow on the meadows was about ten inches deep, and it was still falling in a fine, cordial storm. During the night of the 18th heavy rain fell on the snow, but as the temperature was 34°, the snow-line was only a few hundred feet above the bottom of the Valley, and one had only to climb a little higher than the tops of the pines to get out of the rainstorm into the snowstorm. The streams, instead of being increased in volume by the storm, were diminished, because the snow sponged up part of their waters and choked the smaller tributaries. But about midnight the temperature suddenly rose to 42°, carrying the snow-line far beyond the Valley walls, and next morning Yosemite was rejoicing in a glorious flood. The comparatively warm rain falling on the snow was at first absorbed and held back, and so also was that portion of the snow that the rain melted, and all that was melted by the warm wind, until the whole mass of snow was saturated and became sludgy, and at length slipped and rushed simultaneously from a thousand slopes in wildest extravagance, heaping and swelling flood over flood, and plunging into the Valley in stupendous avalanches.

Awakened by the roar, I looked out and at once recognized the extraordinary character of the storm. The rain was still pouring in torrent abundance and the wind at gale speed was doing all it could with the flood-making rain.

The section of the north wall visible from my cabin was fairly streaked with new falls—wild roaring singers that seemed strangely out of place. Eager to get into the midst of the show, I snatched a piece of bread for breakfast and ran out. The mountain waters, suddenly liberated, seemed to be holding a grand jubilee. The two Sentinel Cascades rivaled the great falls at ordinary stages, and across the Valley by the Three Brothers I caught glimpses of more falls than I could readily count; while the whole Valley throbbed and trembled, and was filled with an awful, massive, solemn, sea-like roar. After gazing a while enchanted with the network of new falls that were adorning and transfiguring every rock in sight, I tried to reach the upper meadows, where the Valley is widest, that I might be able to see the walls on both sides, and thus gain general views. But the river was over its banks and the meadows were flooded, forming an almost

continuous lake dotted with blue sludgy islands, while
innumerable streams roared like lions across my path
and were sweeping forward rocks and logs with tremendous energy over ground where tiny gilias had
been growing but a short time before. Climbing into
the talus slopes, where these savage torrents were
broken among earthquake boulders, I managed to
cross them, and force my way up the Valley to Hutchings' Bridge, where I crossed the river and waded to
the middle of the upper meadow. Here most of the
new falls were in sight, probably the most glorious
assemblage of waterfalls ever displayed from any one
standpoint. On that portion of the south wall between
Hutchings' and the Sentinel there were ten falls
plunging and booming from a height of nearly three
thousand feet, the smallest of which might have been
heard miles away. In the neighborhood of Glacier
Point there were six; between the Three Brothers and
Yosemite Fall, nine; between Yosemite and Royal
Arch Falls, ten; from Washington Column to Mount
Watkins, ten; on the slopes of Half Dome and Clouds
Rest, facing Mirror Lake and Tenaya Canyon, eight;
on the shoulder of Half Dome, facing the Valley,
three; fifty-six new falls occupying the upper end of
the Valley, besides a countless host of silvery threads
gleaming everywhere. In all the Valley there must
have been upwards of a hundred. As if celebrating
some great event, falls and cascades in Yosemite cos-
tume were coming down everywhere from fountain
basins, far and near; and, though newcomers, they
behaved and sang as if they had lived here always.

All summer visitors will remember the comet forms
of the Yosemite Fall and the laces of the Bridal Veil
and Nevada. In the falls of this winter jubilee the lace
forms predominated, but there was no lack of thunder-
toned comets. The lower portion of one of the Sen-

tinel Cascades was composed of two main white torrents with the space between them filled in with chained and beaded gauze of intricate pattern, through the singing threads of which the purplish-gray rock could be dimly seen. The series above Glacier Point was still more complicated in structure, displaying every form that one could imagine water might be dashed and combed and woven into. Those on the north wall between Washington Column and the Royal Arch Fall were so nearly related they formed an almost continuous sheet, and these again were but slightly separated from those about Indian Canyon. The group about the Three Brothers and El Capitan, owing to the topography and cleavage of the cliffs back of them, was more broken and irregular. The Tissiack Cascades[1] were comparatively small, yet sufficient to give that noblest of mountain rocks a glorious voice. In the midst of all this extravagant rejoicing the great Yosemite Fall was scarce heard until about three o'clock in the afternoon. Then I was startled by a sudden thundering crash as if a rock avalanche had come to the help of the roaring waters. This was the flood-wave of Yosemite Creek, which had just arrived, delayed by the distance it had to travel, and by the choking snows of its widespread fountains. Now, with volume tenfold increased beyond its spring-time fullness, it took its place as leader of the glorious choir.

And the winds, too, were singing in wild accord, playing on every tree and rock, surging against the huge brows and domes and outstanding battlements, deflected hither and thither and broken into a thousand cascading, roaring currents in the canyons, and low bass, drumming swirls in the hollows. And these

[1] Tissiack: Half Dome.

again, reacting on the clouds, eroded immense cavern-
ous spaces in their gray depths and swept forward the
resulting detritus in ragged trains like the moraines of
glaciers. These cloud movements in turn published the
work of the winds, giving them a visible body, and
enabling us to trace them. As if endowed with independent motion, a detached cloud would rise hastily
to the very top of the wall as if on some important
errand, examining the faces of the cliffs, and then perhaps as suddenly descend to sweep imposingly along
the meadows, trailing its draggled fringes through the
pines, fondling the waving spires with infinite gentleness, or, gliding behind a grove or a single tree, bringing it into striking relief, as it bowed and waved
in solemn rhythm. Sometimes, as the busy clouds
drooped and condensed or dissolved to misty gauze,
half of the Valley would be suddenly veiled, leaving
here and there some lofty headland cut off from all
visible connection with the walls, looming alone, dim,
spectral, as if belonging to the sky—visitors, like the
new falls, come to take part in the glorious festival.
Thus for two days and nights in measureless extravagance the storm went on, and mostly without specta-
tors, at least of a terrestrial kind. I saw nobody out—
bird, bear, squirrel, or man. Tourists had vanished
months before, and the hotel people and laborers were
out of sight, careful about getting cold, and satisfied
with views from windows. The bears, I suppose, were
in their canyon-boulder dens, the squirrels in their
knot-hole nests, the grouse in close fir groves, and the
small singers in the Indian Canyon chaparral, trying
to keep warm and dry. Strange to say, I did not see
even the water-ouzels, though they must have greatly
enjoyed the storm.

This was the most sublime waterfall flood I ever
saw—clouds, winds, rocks, waters, throbbing together

as one. And then to contemplate what was going on simultaneously with all this in other mountain temples; the Big Tuolumne Canyon—how the white waters and the winds were singing there! And in Hetch Hetchy Valley and the great Kings River yosemite, and in all the other Sierra canyons and valleys from Shasta to the southernmost fountains of the Kern, thousands of rejoicing flood waterfalls chanting together in jubilee dress.

III

SNOWSTORMS

As has been already stated, the first of the great snowstorms that replenish the Yosemite fountains seldom sets in before the end of November. Then, warned by the sky, wide-awake mountaineers, together with the deer and most of the birds, make haste to the lowlands or foothills; and burrowing marmots, mountain beavers, wood-rats, and other small mountain people, go into winter quarters, some of them not again to see the light of day until the general awakening and resurrection of the spring in June or July. The fertile clouds, drooping and condensing in brooding silence, seem to be thoughtfully examining the forests and streams with reference to the work that lies before them. At length, all their plans perfected, tufted flakes and single starry crystals come in sight, solemnly swirling and glinting to their blessed appointed places; and soon the busy throng fills the sky and makes darkness like night. The first heavy fall is usually from about two to four feet in depth; then with intervals of days or weeks of bright weather storm succeeds storm, heaping snow on snow, until thirty to fifty feet has fallen. But on account of its settling and compacting, and waste from melting and evaporation, the average depth actually found at any time seldom exceeds ten feet in the forest regions, or fifteen feet along the slopes of the summit peaks. After snowstorms come avalanches, varying greatly in form, size, behavior and in the songs they sing; some on the smooth slopes of the mountains are short and broad; others long and river-like in the side canyons of yosemites and in the main canyons, flowing in regular channels and booming like waterfalls, while countless smaller ones fall everywhere from laden trees and rocks and lofty canyon walls. Most delightful it is to stand in the middle of Yosemite on still clear mornings after snowstorms and watch the throng of avalanches as they come down, rejoicing, to their places, whispering, thrilling like birds, or booming and roaring like thunder. The noble yellow pines stand hushed and motionless as if under a spell until the morning sunshine begins to sift through their laden spires; then the dense masses on the ends of the leafy branches begin to shift and fall, those from the upper branches striking the lower ones in succession, enveloping each tree in a hollow conical avalanche of fairy fineness; while the relieved branches spring up and wave with startling effect in the general stillness, as if each tree was moving of its own volition. Hundreds of broad cloud-shaped masses may also be seen, leaping over the brows of the cliffs from great heights, descending at first with regular avalanche speed until, worn into dust by friction, they float in front of the precipices like irised clouds. Those which descend from the brow of El Capitan are particularly fine; but most of the great Yosemite avalanches flow in regular channels like cascades and waterfalls. When the snow first gives way on the upper slopes of their basins, a dull rushing, rumbling sound is heard which rapidly increases and seems to draw nearer with appalling intensity of tone. Presently the white flood comes bounding into sight over bosses and sheer places, leaping from bench to bench, spreading and narrowing and throwing off clouds of whirling dust like the spray of foaming cataracts. Compared with waterfalls and cascades, avalanches

are short-lived, few of them lasting more than a minute or two, and the sharp, clashing sounds so common
in falling water are mostly wanting; but in their low
massy thunder-tones and purple-tinged whiteness, and
in their dress, gait, gestures and general behavior, they
are much alike.

AVALANCHES

Besides these common after-storm avalanches that
are to be found not only in the Yosemite but in all the
deep, sheer-walled canyons of the range there are
two other important kinds, which may be called annual and century avalanches, which still further enrich the scenery. The only place about the Valley
where one may be sure to see the annual kind is on
the north slope of Clouds Rest. They are composed of
heavy, compacted snow, which has been subjected to
frequent alternations of freezing and thawing. They
are developed on canyon and mountain-sides at an
elevation of from nine to ten thousand feet, where the
slopes are inclined at an angle too low to shed off the
dry winter snow, and which accumulates until the
spring thaws sap their foundations and make them
slippery; then away in grand style go the ponderous
icy masses without any fine snow-dust. Those of
Clouds Rest descend like thunderbolts for more than
a mile.

The great century avalanches and the kind that
mow wide swaths through the upper forests occur on
mountain-sides about ten or twelve thousand feet
high, where under ordinary weather conditions the
snow accumulated from winter to winter lies at rest
for many years, allowing trees, fifty to a hundred feet
high, to grow undisturbed on the slopes beneath them.
On their way down through the woods they seldom
fail to make a perfectly clean sweep, stripping off the

soil as well as the trees, clearing paths two or three hundred yards wide from the timberline to the glacier meadows or lakes, and piling their uprooted trees, head downward, in rows along the sides of the gaps like lateral moraines. Scars and broken branches of the trees standing on the sides of the gaps record the depth of the overwhelming flood; and when we come to count the annual wood-rings on the uprooted trees we learn that some of these immense avalanches occur only once in a century or even at still wider intervals.

A RIDE ON AN AVALANCHE

Few Yosemite visitors ever see snow avalanches and fewer still know the exhilaration of riding on them. In all my mountaineering I have enjoyed only one avalanche ride, and the start was so sudden and the end came so soon I had but little time to think of the danger that attends this sort of travel, though at such times one thinks fast. One fine Yosemite morning after a heavy snowfall, being eager to see as many avalanches as possible and wide views of the forest and summit peaks in their new white robes before the sunshine had time to change them, I set out early to climb by a side canyon to the top of a commanding ridge a little over three thousand feet above the Valley. On account of the looseness of the snow that blocked the canyon I knew the climb would require a long time, some three or four hours as I estimated; but it proved far more difficult than I had anticipated. Most of the way I sank waist deep, almost out of sight in some places. After spending the whole day to within half an hour or so of sundown, I was still several hundred feet below the summit. Then my hopes were reduced to getting up in time to see the sunset. But I was not to get summit views of any sort that day, for

deep trampling near the canyon head, where the snow
was strained, started an avalanche, and I was swished
down to the foot of the canyon as if by enchantment.
The wallowing ascent had taken nearly all day, the
descent only about a minute. When the avalanche
started I threw myself on my back and spread my
arms to try to keep from sinking. Fortunately, though
the grade of the canyon is very steep, it is not interrupted by precipices large enough to cause outbounding or free plunging. On no part of the rush was I
buried. I was only moderately imbedded on the surface or at times a little below it, and covered with a
veil of back-streaming dust particles; and as the whole
mass beneath and about me joined in the flight there
was no friction, though I was tossed here and there
and lurched from side to side. When the avalanche
swedged and came to rest I found myself on top of
the crumpled pile without a bruise or scar. This was
a fine experience. Hawthorne says somewhere that
steam has spiritualized travel; though unspiritual
smells, smoke, etc., still attend steam travel. This
flight in what might be called a milky way of snow-
stars was the most spiritual and exhilarating of all the
modes of motion I have ever experienced. Elijah's
flight in a chariot of fire could hardly have been more
gloriously exciting.

THE STREAMS IN OTHER SEASONS

In the spring, after all the avalanches are down and
the snow is melting fast, then all the Yosemite streams,
from their fountains to their falls, sing their grandest
songs. Countless rills make haste to the rivers, running
and singing soon after sunrise, louder and louder with
increasing volume until sundown; then they gradually
fail through the frosty hours of the night. In this way
the volume of the upper branches of the river is nearly

doubled during the day, rising and falling as regularly as the tides of the sea. Then the Merced overflows its banks, flooding the meadows, sometimes almost from wall to wall in some places, beginning to rise towards sundown just when the streams on the fountains are beginning to diminish, the difference in time of the daily rise and fall being caused by the distance the upper flood streams have to travel before reaching the Valley. In the warmest weather they seem fairly to shout for joy and clash their upleaping waters together like clapping of hands; racing down the canyons with white manes flying in glorious exuberance of strength, compelling huge, sleeping boulders to wake up and join in their dance and song, to swell their exulting chorus.

In early summer, after the flood season, the Yosemite streams are in their prime, running crystal clear, deep and full but not overflowing their banks—about as deep through the night as the day, the difference in volume so marked in spring being now too slight to be noticed. Nearly all the weather is cloudless and everything is at its brightest—lake, river, garden and forest with all their life. Most of the plants are in full flower. The blessed ouzels have built their mossy huts and are now singing their best songs with the streams.

In tranquil, mellow autumn, when the year's work is about done and the fruits are ripe, birds and seeds out of their nests, and all the landscape is glowing like a benevolent countenance, then the streams are at their lowest ebb, with scarce a memory left of their wild spring floods. The small tributaries that do not reach back to the lasting snow fountains of the summit peaks shrink to whispering, tinkling currents. After the snow is gone from the basins, excepting occasional thunder-showers, they are now fed only by small springs whose waters are mostly evaporated in passing over miles of warm pavements, and in feeling their way slowly from pool to pool through the midst of boulders and sand. Even the main rivers are so low they may easily be forded, and their grand falls and cascades, now gentle and approachable, have waned to sheets of embroidery.

IV

SNOW BANNERS

But it is on the mountain tops, when they are laden with loose, dry snow and swept by a gale from the north, that the most magnificent storm scenery is displayed. The peaks along the axis of the Range are then decorated with resplendent banners, some of them more than a mile long, shining, streaming, waving with solemn exuberant enthusiasm as if celebrating some surpassingly glorious event.

The snow of which these banners are made falls on the high Sierra in most extravagant abundance, sometimes to a depth of fifteen or twenty feet, coming from the fertile clouds not in large tangled flakes such as one oftentimes sees in Yosemite, seldom even in complete crystals, for many of the starry blossoms fall before they are ripe, while most of those that attain perfect development as six-petaled flowers are more or less broken by glinting and chafing against one another on the way down to their work. This dry frosty snow is prepared for the grand banner-waving celebrations by the action of the wind. Instead of at once finding rest like that which falls into the tranquil depths of the forest, it is shoved and rolled and beaten against boulders and out-jutting rocks, swirled in pits and hollows like sand in river potholes, and ground into sparkling dust. And when storm winds find this snow-dust in a loose condition on the slopes above the timberline they toss it back into the sky and sweep it onward from peak to peak in the form of smooth regu-

lar banners, or in cloudy drifts, according to the velocity and direction of the wind, and the conformation
of the slopes over which it is driven. While thus flying
through the air a small portion escapes from the mountains to the sky as vapor; but far the greater part is at
length locked fast in bossy overcurling cornices along
the ridges, or in stratified sheets in the glacier cirques,
some of it to replenish the small residual glaciers and
remain silent and rigid for centuries before it is finally
melted and sent singing down home to the sea.

But, though snow-dust and storm-winds abound on
the mountains, regular shapely banners are, for causes
we shall presently see, seldom produced. During the
five winters that I spent in Yosemite I made many
excursions to high points above the walls in all kinds
of weather to see what was going on outside; from all
my lofty outlooks I saw only one banner-storm that
seemed in every way perfect. This was in the winter
of 1873, when the snow-laden peaks were swept by a
powerful norther. I was awakened early in the morning by a wild storm-wind and of course I had to make
haste to the middle of the Valley to enjoy it. Rugged
torrents and avalanches from the main wind-flood
overhead were roaring down the side canyons and
over the cliffs, arousing the rocks and the trees and
the streams alike into glorious hurrahing enthusiasm,
shaking the whole Valley into one huge song. Yet in-
conceivable as it must seem even to those who love all
Nature's wildness, the storm was telling its story on
the mountains in still grander characters.

A WONDERFUL WINTER SCENE

I had long been anxious to study some points in the
structure of the ice-hill at the foot of the Upper Yosemite Fall, but, as I have already explained, blinding
spray had hitherto prevented me from getting suffi-

ciently near it. This morning the entire body of the
fall was oftentimes torn into gauzy strips and blown
horizontally along the face of the cliff, leaving the ice-
hill dry; and while making my way to the top of Fern
Ledge to seize so favorable an opportunity to look
down its throat, the peaks of the Merced group came
in sight over the shoulder of the South Dome, each
waving a white glowing banner against the dark blue
sky, as regular in form and firm and fine in texture as
if it were made of silk. So rare and splendid a picture,
of course, smothered everything else and I at once
began to scramble and wallow up the snow-choked
Indian Canyon to a ridge about 8000 feet high, commanding a general view of the main summits along the
axis of the range, feeling assured I should find them
bannered still more gloriously; nor was I in the least
disappointed. I reached the top of the ridge in four
or five hours, and through an opening in the woods
the most imposing wind-storm effect I ever beheld
came full in sight; unnumbered mountains rising
sharply into the cloudless sky, their bases solid white,
their sides plashed with snow, like ocean rocks with
foam, and on every summit a magnificent silvery banner, from two thousand to six thousand feet in length,
slender at the point of attachment, and widening
gradually until about a thousand or fifteen hundred
feet in breadth, and as shapely and as substantial looking in texture as the banners of the finest silk, all
streaming and waving free and clear in the sun-glow
with nothing to blur the sublime picture they made.

Fancy yourself standing beside me on this Yosemite
ridge. There is a strange garish glitter in the air and
the gale drives wildly overhead, but you feel nothing
of its violence, for you are looking out through a sheltered opening in the woods, as through a window. In
the immediate foreground there is a forest of silver

firs, their foliage warm yellow-green, and the snow beneath them is strewn with their plumes, plucked off by the storm; and beyond a broad, ridgy, canyon-furrowed, dome-dotted middle ground, darkened here and there with belts of pines, you behold the lofty snow-laden mountains in glorious array, waving their banners with jubilant enthusiasm as if shouting aloud for joy. They are twenty miles away, but you would not wish them nearer, for every feature is distinct, and the whole wonderful show is seen in its right proportions, like a painting on the sky.

And now after this general view, mark how sharply the ribs and buttresses and summits of the mountains are defined, excepting the portions veiled by the banners; how gracefully and nobly the banners are waving in accord with the throbbing of the wind-flood; how trimly each is attached to the very summit of its peak like a streamer at a mast-head; how bright and glowing white they are, and how finely their fading fringes are penciled on the sky! See how solid white and opaque they are at the point of attachment and how filmy and translucent toward the end, so that the parts of the peaks past which they are streaming look dim as if seen through a veil of ground glass. And see how some of the longest of the banners on the highest peaks are streaming perfectly free from peak to peak across intervening notches or passes, while others overlap and partly hide one another.

As to their formation, we find that the main causes of the wondrous beauty and perfection of those we are looking at are the favorable direction and force of the wind, the abundance of snow-dust, and the form of the north sides of the peaks. In general, the north sides are concave in both their horizontal and vertical sections, having been sculptured into this shape by the residual glaciers that lingered in the protecting northern shadows, while the sun-beaten south sides, having never been subjected to this kind of glaciation, are convex or irregular. It is essential, therefore, not only that the wind should move with great velocity and steadiness to supply a sufficiently copious and continuous stream of snow-dust, but that it should come from the north. No perfect banner is ever hung on the Sierra peaks by the south wind. Had the gale today blown from the south, leaving the other conditions unchanged, only swirling, interfering, cloudy drifts would have been produced; for the snow, instead of being spouted straight up and over the tops of the peaks in condensed currents to be drawn out as streamers, would have been driven over the convex southern slopes from peak to peak like white pearly fog.

It appears, therefore, that shadows in great part determine not only the forms of lofty ice mountains, but also those of the snow banners that the wild winds hang upon them.

EARTHQUAKE STORMS

The avalanche taluses, leaning against the walls at intervals of a mile or two, are among the most striking and interesting of the secondary features of the Valley. They are from about three to five hundred feet high, made up of huge, angular, well-preserved, unshifting boulders, and instead of being slowly weathered from the cliffs like ordinary taluses, they were all formed suddenly and simultaneously by a great earthquake that occurred at least three centuries ago. And though thus hurled into existence in a few seconds or minutes, they are the least changeable of all the Sierra soil-beds. Excepting those which were launched directly into the channels of swift rivers, scarcely one of their wedged and interlacing boulders has moved

since the day of their creation; and though mostly
made up of huge blocks of granite, many of them
from ten to fifty feet cube, weighing thousands of tons
with only a few small chips, trees and shrubs make out
to live and thrive on them and even delicate herbaceous plants—draperia, collomia, zauschneria, etc.,
soothing and coloring their wild rugged slopes with
gardens and groves.

I was long in doubt on some points concerning the
origin of these taluses. Plainly enough they were derived from the cliffs above them, because they are of
the size of scars on the wall, the rough angular surface
of which contrasts with the rounded, glaciated, un-
fractured parts. It was plain, too, that instead of being
made up of material slowly and gradually weathered
from the cliffs like ordinary taluses, almost every one
of them had been formed suddenly in a single avalanche, and had not been increased in size during the
last three or four centuries, for trees three or four hundred years old are growing on them, some standing at
the top close to the wall without a bruise or broken
branch, showing that scarcely a single boulder had
ever fallen among them. Furthermore, all these taluses
throughout the range seemed by the trees and lichens
growing on them to be of the same age. All the phenomena thus pointed straight to a grand ancient earthquake. But for years I left the question open, and
went on from canyon to canyon, observing again and
again; measuring the heights of taluses throughout the
range on both flanks, and the variations in the angles
of their surface slopes; studying the way their boulders
had been assorted and related and brought to rest,
and their correspondence in size with the cleavage
joints of the cliffs from whence they were derived,
cautious about making up my mind. But at last all
doubt as to their formation vanished.

At half-past two o'clock of a moonlit morning in March, I was awakened by a tremendous earthquake, and though I had never before enjoyed a storm of this sort, the strange thrilling motion could not be mistaken, and I ran out of my cabin, both glad and frightened, shouting, "A noble earthquake! A noble earthquake!" feeling sure I was going to learn something. The shocks were so violent and varied, and succeeded one another so closely, that I had to balance myself carefully in walking as if on the deck of a ship among waves, and it seemed impossible that the high cliffs of the Valley could escape being shattered. In particular, I feared that the sheer-fronted Sentinel Rock, towering above my cabin, would be shaken down, and I took shelter back of a large yellow pine, hoping that it might protect me from at least the smaller outbounding boulders. For a minute or two the shocks became more and more violent—flashing horizontal thrusts mixed with a few twists and battering, explosive, up-heaving jolts,—as if Nature were wrecking her Yosemite temple, and getting ready to build a still better one.

I was now convinced before a single boulder had fallen that earthquakes were the talus-makers and positive proof soon came. It was a calm moonlight night, and no sound was heard for the first minute or so, save low, muffled, underground, bubbling rumblings, and the whispering and rustling of the agitated trees, as if Nature were holding her breath. Then, suddenly, out of the strange silence and strange motion there came a tremendous roar. The Eagle Rock on the south wall, about a half a mile up the Valley, gave way and I saw it falling in thousands of the great boulders I had so long been studying, pouring to the Valley floor in a free curve luminous from friction, making a terribly sublime spectacle—an arc of glowing, passionate fire, fifteen hundred feet span, as true

in form and as serene in beauty as a rainbow in the
midst of the stupendous, roaring rock-storm. The
sound was so tremendously deep and broad and earnest, the whole earth like a living creature seemed to
have at last found a voice and to be calling to her
sister planets. In trying to tell something of the size of
this awful sound it seems to me that if all the thunder
of all the storms I had ever heard were condensed into
one roar it would not equal this rock-roar at the birth
of a mountain talus. Think, then, of the roar that arose
to heaven at the simultaneous birth of all the thousands of ancient canyon-taluses throughout the length
and breadth of the range!

The first severe shocks were soon over, and eager
to examine the new-born talus I ran up the Valley in
the moonlight and climbed upon it before the huge
blocks, after their fiery flight, had come to complete
rest. They were slowly settling into their places, chafing, grating against one another, groaning, and whispering; but no motion was visible except in a stream
of small fragments pattering down the face of the cliff.
A cloud of dust particles, lighted by the moon, floated
out across the whole breadth of the Valley, forming a
ceiling that lasted until after sunrise, and the air was
filled with the odor of crushed Douglas spruces from
a grove that had been mowed down and mashed like
weeds.

After the ground began to calm I ran across the
meadow to the river to see in what direction it was
flowing and was glad to find that *down* the Valley
was still down. Its waters were muddy from portions
of its banks having given way, but it was flowing
around its curves and over its ripples and shallows
with ordinary tones and gestures. The mud would
soon be cleared away and the raw slips on the banks

would be the only visible record of the shaking it suffered.

The Upper Yosemite Fall, glowing white in the moonlight, seemed to know nothing of the earthquake, manifesting no change in form or voice, as far as I could see or hear.

After a second startling shock, about half-past three o'clock, the ground continued to tremble gently, and smooth, hollow rumbling sounds, not always distinguishable from the rounded, bumping, explosive tones of the falls, came from deep in the mountains in a northern direction.

The few Indians fled from their huts to the middle of the Valley, fearing that angry spirits were trying to kill them; and, as I afterward learned, most of the Yosemite tribe, who were spending the winter at their village on Bull Creek forty miles away, were so terrified that they ran into the river and washed themselves,—getting themselves clean enough to say their prayers, I suppose, or to die. I asked Dick, one of the Indians with whom I was acquainted, "What made the ground shake and jump so much?" He only shook his head and said, "No good. No good," and looked appealingly to me to give him hope that his life was to be spared.

In the morning I found the few white settlers assembled in front of the old Hutchings Hotel comparing notes and meditating flight to the lowlands, seemingly as sorely frightened as the Indians. Shortly after sunrise a low, blunt, muffled rumbling, like distant thunder, was followed by another series of shocks, which, though not nearly so severe as the first, made the cliffs and domes tremble like jelly, and the big pines and oaks thrill and swish and wave their branches with startling effect. Then the talkers were suddenly hushed, and the solemnity on their faces was sublime. One in particular of these winter neighbors, a somewhat speculative thinker with whom I had often conversed, was a firm believer in the cataclysmic origin of the Valley; and I now jokingly remarked that his wild tumble-down-and-engulfment hypothesis might soon be proved, since these underground rumblings and shakings might be the forerunners of another Yosemite-making cataclysm, which would perhaps double the depth of the Valley by swallowing the floor, leaving the ends of the roads and trails dangling three or four thousand feet in the air. Just then came the third series of shocks, and it was fine to see how awfully silent and solemn he became. His belief in the existence of a mysterious abyss, into which the suspended floor of the Valley and all the domes and battlements of the walls might at any moment go roaring down, mightily troubled him. To diminish his fears and laugh him into something like reasonable faith, I said, "Come, cheer up; smile a little and clap your hands, now that kind Mother Earth is trotting us on her knee to amuse us and make us good." But the well-meant joke seemed irreverent and utterly failed, as if only prayerful terror could rightly belong to the wild beauty-making business. Even after all the heavier shocks were over I could do nothing to reassure him. On the contrary, he handed me the keys of his little store to keep, saying that with a companion of like mind he was going to the lowlands to stay until the fate of poor, trembling Yosemite was settled. In vain I rallied them on their fears, calling attention to the strength of the granite walls of our Valley home, the very best and solidest masonry in the world, and less likely to collapse and sink than the sedimentary lowlands to which they were looking for safety; and saying that in any case they sometime would have to die, and so grand a burial was not to be slighted. But they were too seriously panic-stricken to get comfort from anything I could say.

During the third severe shock the trees were so violently shaken that the birds flew out with frightened cries. In particular, I noticed two robins flying in terror from a leafless oak, the branches of which swished and quivered as if struck by a heavy battering-ram. Exceedingly interesting were the flashing and quivering of the elastic needles of the pines in the sunlight and the waving up and down of the branches while the trunks stood rigid. There was no swaying, waving or swirling as in wind-storms, but quick, quivering jerks, and at times the heavy tasseled branches moved as if they had all been pressed down against the trunk and suddenly let go, to spring up and vibrate until they came to rest again. Only the owls seemed to be undisturbed. Before the rumbling echoes had died away a hollow-voiced owl began to hoot in philosophical tranquillity from near the edge of the new talus as if nothing extraordinary had occurred, although, perhaps, he was curious to know what all the noise was about. His "hoot-too-hoot-too-whoo" might have meant, "what's a' the steer, kimmer?"

It was long before the Valley found perfect rest. The rocks trembled more or less every day for over two months, and I kept a bucket of water on my table to learn what I could of the movements. The blunt thunder in the depths of the mountains was usually followed by sudden jarring, horizontal thrusts from the northward, often succeeded by twisting, upjolting movements. More than a month after the first great shock, when I was standing on a fallen tree up the Valley near Lamon's winter cabin, I heard a distinct bubbling thunder from the direction of Tenaya Canyon. Carlo, a large intelligent St. Bernard dog standing beside me, seemed greatly astonished, and looked in-

tently in that direction with mouth open and uttered
a low *Wouf!* as if saying, "What's that?" He must have
known that it was not thunder, though like it. The air
was perfectly still, not the faintest breath of wind perceptible, and a fine, mellow, sunny hush pervaded
everything, in the midst of which came that subter-
ranean thunder. Then, while we gazed and listened,
came the corresponding shocks, distinct as if some
mighty hand had shaken the ground. After the sharp
horizontal jars died away, they were followed by a
gentle rocking and undulating of the ground so distinct that Carlo looked at the log on which he was
standing to see who was shaking it. It was the season
of flooded meadows and the pools about me, calm as
sheets of glass, were suddenly thrown into low ruffling
waves.

Judging by its effects, this Yosemite, or Inyo earthquake, as it is sometimes called, was gentle as compared with the one that gave rise to the grand talus
system of the range and did so much for the canyon
scenery. Nature, usually so deliberate in her operations, then created, as we have seen, a new set of
features, simply by giving the mountains a shake—
changing not only the high peaks and cliffs, but the
streams. As soon as these rock avalanches fell, the
streams began to sing new songs; for in many places
thousands of boulders were hurled into their channels,
roughening and half-damming them, compelling the
waters to surge and roar in rapids where before they
glided smoothly. Some of the streams were completely
dammed; driftwood, leaves, etc., gradually filling the
interstices between the boulders, thus giving rise to
lakes and level reaches; and these again, after being
gradually filled in, were changed to meadows, through
which the streams are now silently meandering; while
at the same time some of the taluses took the places

of old meadows and groves. Thus rough places were made smooth, and smooth places rough. But, on the whole, by what at first sight seemed pure confounded confusion and ruin, the landscapes were enriched; for gradually every talus was covered with groves and gardens, and made a finely proportioned and ornamental base for the cliffs. In this work of beauty, every boulder is prepared and measured and put in its place more thoughtfully than are the stones of temples. If for a moment you are inclined to regard these taluses as mere draggled, chaotic dumps, climb to the top of one of them, and run down without any haggling, puttering hesitation, boldly jumping from boulder to boulder with even speed. You will then find your feet playing a tune, and quickly discover the music and poetry of these magnificent rock piles—a fine lesson; and all Nature's wildness tells the same story—the shocks and outbursts of earthquakes, volcanoes, geysers, roaring, thundering waves and floods, the silent uprush of sap in plants, storms of every sort—each and all are the orderly beauty-making love-beats of Nature's heart.[1]

[1] Muir's description is of the great Inyo earthquake of March 26, 1872, which caused considerable damage and many deaths in the town of Lone Pine, in the Owens Valley southeast of Yosemite. The intensity of the seismic disturbance is believed to have been at least equal to that of the San Francisco earthquake of 1906, 8.25 on the Gutenberg-Richter scale.

V

THE TREES OF THE VALLEY

The most influential of the Valley trees is the yellow pine (*Pinus ponderosa*). It attains its noblest dimensions on beds of water-washed, coarsely-stratified moraine material, between the talus slopes and meadows, dry on the surface, well-watered below and where not too closely assembled in groves the branches reach nearly to the ground, forming grand spires 200 to 220 feet in height. The largest that I have measured is standing alone almost opposite the Sentinel Rock, or a little to the westward of it. It is a little over eight feet in diameter and about 220 feet high. Climbing these grand trees, especially when they are waving and singing in worship in wind-storms, is a glorious experience. Ascending from the lowest branch to the topmost is like stepping up stairs through a blaze of white light, every needle thrilling and shining as if with religious ecstasy.

Unfortunately there are but few sugar pines in the Valley, though in the Kings yosemite they are in glorious abundance. The incense cedar (*Libocedrus decurrens*) with cinnamon-colored bark and yellow-green foliage is one of the most interesting of the Yosemite trees. Some of them are 150 feet high, from six to ten feet in diameter, and they are never out of sight as you saunter among the yellow pines. Their bright brown shafts and towers of flat, frond-like branches make a striking feature of the landscapes throughout all the seasons. In midwinter, when most of the other trees are asleep, this cedar puts forth its

flowers in millions,—the pistillate pale green and in-
conspicuous, but the staminate bright yellow, tingeing
all the branches and making the trees as they stand in
the snow look like gigantic goldenrods. The branches,
outspread in flat plumes and, beautifully fronded,
sweep gracefully downward and outward, except
those near the top, which aspire; the lowest, especially
in youth and middle age, droop to the ground, overlapping one another, shedding off rain and snow like
shingles, and making fine tents for birds and campers.
This tree frequently lives more than a thousand years
and is well worthy its place beside the great pines and
the Douglas spruce.[1]

The two largest specimens I know of the Douglas
spruce, about eight feet in diameter, are growing at
the foot of the Liberty Cap near the Nevada Fall, and
on the terminal moraine of the small residual glacier
that lingered in the shady Illilouette Canyon.

After the conifers, the most important of the Yosemite trees are the oaks, two species; the California live-
oak (*Quercus agrifolia*),[2] with black trunks, reaching
a thickness of from four to nearly seven feet, wide
spreading branches and bright deeply-scalloped
leaves. It occupies the greater part of the broad sandy
flats of the upper end of the Valley, and is the species
that yields the acorns so highly prized by the Indians
and woodpeckers.

The other species is the mountain live-oak, or gold-
cup oak (*Quercus chrysolepis*), a sturdy mountaineer
of a tree, growing mostly on the earthquake taluses
and benches of the sunny north wall of the Valley.
In tough, unwedgeable, knotty strength, it is the oak
of oaks, a magnificent tree.

The largest and most picturesque specimen in the
Valley is near the foot of the Tenaya Fall, a romantic

[1] Douglas fir.
[2] Muir means California black oak, *Q. Kelloggii.*

spot seldom seen on account of the rough trouble of getting to it. It is planted on three huge boulders and yet manages to draw sufficient moisture and food from this craggy soil to maintain itself in good health. It is twenty feet in circumference, measured above a large branch between three and four feet in diameter that has been broken off. The main knotty trunk seems to be made up of craggy granite boulders like those on which it stands, being about the same color as the mossy, lichened boulders and about as rough. Two moss-lined caves near the ground open back into the trunk, one on the north side, the other on the west, forming picturesque, romantic seats. The largest of the main branches is eighteen feet and nine inches in circumference, and some of the long pendulous branchlets droop over the stream at the foot of the fall where it is gray with spray. The leaves are glossy yellow-green, ever in motion from the wind from the fall. It is a fine place to dream in, with falls, cascades, cool rocks lined with hypnum three inches thick; shaded with maple, dogwood, alder, willow; grand clumps of lady-ferns where no hand may touch them; light filtering through translucent leaves; oaks fifty feet high; lilies eight feet high in a filled lake basin near by, and the finest libocedrus groves and tallest ferns and goldenrods.

In the main river canyon below the Vernal Fall and on the shady south side of the Valley there are a few groves of the silver fir (*Abies concolor*), and superb forests of the magnificent species around the rim of the Valley.

On the tops of the domes is found the sturdy, storm-enduring red cedar (*Juniperus occidentalis*).[3] It never makes anything like a forest here, but stands out separate and independent in the wind, clinging by slight

[3] Sierra juniper.

joints to the rock, with scarce a handful of soil in sight of it, seeming to depend chiefly on snow and air for nourishment, and yet it has maintained tough health on this diet for two thousand years or more. The largest hereabouts are from five to six feet in diameter and fifty feet in height.

The principal river-side trees are poplar,[4] alder, willow, broad-leaved maple, and Nuttall's flowering dogwood. The poplar (*Populus trichocarpa*), often called balm-of-Gilead from the gum on its buds, is a tall tree, towering above its companions and gracefully embowering the banks of the river. Its abundant foliage turns bright yellow in the fall, and the Indian-summer sunshine sifts through it in delightful tones over the slow-gliding waters when they are at their lowest ebb.

Some of the involucres of the flowering dogwood measure six to eight inches in diameter, and the whole tree when in flower looks as if covered with snow. In the spring when the streams are in flood it is the whitest of trees. In Indian summer the leaves become bright crimson, making a still grander show than the flowers.

The broad-leaved maple and mountain maple are found mostly in the cool canyons at the head of the Valley, spreading their branches in beautiful arches over the foaming streams.

Scattered here and there are a few other trees, mostly small—the mountain mahogany, cherry, chestnut-oak, and laurel.[5] The California nutmeg (*Torreya californica*), a handsome evergreen, belonging to the yew family, forms small groves near the cascades a mile or two below the foot of the Valley.

[4] Black cottonwood, *Populus trichocarpa*.
[5] Mountain mahogany: *Cercocarpus betuloides*. Cherry: probably *Prunus demissa*. Chestnut-oak: probably chinquapin, *Castanopsis sempervirens*. Laurel: *Umbellularia californica*.

VI

THE FOREST TREES IN GENERAL

For the use of the ever-increasing number of Yosemite visitors who make extensive excursions into the
mountains beyond the Valley, a sketch of the forest
trees in general will probably be found useful. The
different species are arranged in zones and sections,
which brings the forest as a whole within the compre-
hension of every observer. These species are always
found as controlled by the climates of different elevations, by soil and by the comparative strength of each
species in taking and holding possession of the ground;
and so appreciable are these relations the traveler
need never be at a loss in determining within a few
hundred feet his elevation above sea-level by the trees
alone; for, notwithstanding some of the species range
upward for several thousand feet and all pass one
another more or less, yet even those species possessing
the greatest vertical range are available in measuring
the elevation; inasmuch as they take on new forms
corresponding with variations in altitude. Entering the
lower fringe of the forest composed of Douglas oaks
and Sabine pines, the trees grow so far apart that not
one-twentieth of the surface of the ground is in shade
at noon. After advancing fifteen or twenty miles towards Yosemite and making an ascent of from two to
three thousand feet you reach the lower margin of the
main pine belt, composed of great sugar pine, yellow
pine, incense cedar and sequoia. Next you come to
the magnificent silver-fir belt and lastly to the upper

pine belt, which sweeps up to the feet of the summit peaks in a dwarfed fringe, to a height of from ten to twelve thousand feet. That this general order of distribution depends on climate as affected by height above the sea, is seen at once, but there are other harmonies that become manifest only after observation and study. One of the most interesting of these is the arrangement of the forest in long curving bands, braided together into lace-like patterns in some places and outspread in charming variety. The key to these striking arrangements is the system of ancient glaciers; where they flowed the trees followed, tracing their courses along the sides of canyons, over ridges, and high plateaus. The cedar of Lebanon, said Sir Joseph Hooker, occurs upon one of the moraines of an ancient glacier. All the forests of the Sierra are growing upon moraines, but moraines vanish like the glaciers that make them. Every storm that falls upon them wastes them, carrying away their decaying, disintegrating material into new formations, until they are no longer recognizable without tracing their transitional forms down the range from those still in process of formation in some places through those that are more and more ancient and more obscured by vegetation and all kinds of post-glacial weathering. It appears, therefore, that the Sierra forests indicate the extent and positions of ancient moraines as well as they do belts of climate.

One will have no difficulty in knowing the Nut Pine (*Pinus Sabiniana*),[1] for it is the first conifer met in ascending the range from the west, springing up here and there among Douglas oaks and thickets of ceanothus and manzanita; its extreme upper limit being about 4000 feet above the sea, its lower about from 500 to 800 feet. It is remarkable for its loose, airy,

[1] Digger pine.

wide-branching habit, and thin gray foliage. Full-
grown specimens are from forty to fifty feet in height
and from two to three feet in diameter. The trunk
usually divides into three or four main branches about
fifteen or twenty feet from the ground that, after bearing away from one another, shoot straight up and form
separate summits. Their slender, grayish needles are
from eight to twelve inches long, and inclined to
droop, contrasting with the rigid, dark-colored trunk
and branches. No other tree of my acquaintance so
substantial in its body has foliage so thin and pervious
to the light. The cones are from five to eight inches
long and about as large in thickness; rich chocolate-
brown in color and protected by strong, down-curving
hooks which terminate the scales. Nevertheless the
little Douglas squirrel can open them. Indians climb
the trees like bears and beat off the cones or reck-
lessly cut off the more fruitful branches with hatch-
ets, while the squaws gather and roast them until
the scales open sufficiently to allow the hard-shell
seeds to be beaten out. The curious little *Pinus at-
tenuata*[2] is found at an elevation of from 1500 to
3000 feet, growing in close groves and belts. It is exceedingly slender and graceful, although trees that
chance to stand alone send out very long, curved
branches, making a striking contrast to the ordinary
grove form. The foliage is of the same peculiar gray-
green color as that of the nut pine, and is worn about
as loosely, so that the body of the tree is scarcely obscured by it. At the age of seven or eight years it begins to bear cones in whorls on the main axis, and as
they never fall off, the trunk is soon picturesquely
dotted with them. Branches also soon become fruitful.
The average size of the tree is about thirty or forty
feet in height and twelve to fourteen inches in diame-

[2] Knobcone pine.

ter. The cones are about four inches long, and covered with a sort of varnish and gum, rendering them impervious to moisture.

No observer can fail to notice the admirable adaptation of this curious pine to the fire-swept regions where alone it is found. After a running fire has scorched and killed it the cones open and the ground beneath it is then sown broadcast with all the seeds ripened during its whole life. Then up spring a crowd of bright, hopeful seedlings, giving beauty for ashes in lavish abundance.

THE SUGAR PINE, KING OF PINE TREES

Of all the world's eighty or ninety species of pine trees, the Sugar Pine (*Pinus Lambertiana*) is king, surpassing all others, not merely in size but in lordly beauty and majesty. In the Yosemite region it grows at an elevation of from 3000 to 7000 feet above the sea and attains most perfect development at a height of about 5000 feet. The largest specimens are commonly about 220 feet high and from six to eight feet in diameter four feet from the ground, though some grand old patriarch may be met here and there that has enjoyed six or eight centuries of storms and attained a thickness of ten or even twelve feet, still sweet and fresh in every fiber. The trunk is a remarkably smooth, round, delicately-tapered shaft, straight and regular as if turned in a lathe, mostly without limbs, purplish brown in color and usually enlivened with tufts of a yellow lichen. Toward the head of this magnificent column long branches sweep gracefully outward and downward, sometimes forming a palm-like crown, but far more impressive than any palm crown I ever beheld. The needles are about three inches long in fasicles of five, and arranged in rather close tassels at the ends of slender branchlets that

clothe the long outsweeping limbs. How well they sing
in the wind, and how strikingly harmonious an effect
is made by the long cylindrical cones, depending
loosely from the ends of the long branches! The cones
are about fifteen to eighteen inches long, and three in
diameter; green, shaded with dark purple on their sun-
ward sides. They are ripe in September and October
of the second year from the flower. Then the flat, thin
scales open and the seeds take wing, but the empty
cones become still more beautiful and effective as dec-
orations, for their diameter is nearly doubled by the
spreading of the scales, and their color changes to yel-
lowish brown while they remain, swinging on the tree
all the following winter and summer, and continue ef-
fectively beautiful even on the ground many years
after they fall. The wood is deliciously fragrant, fine in
grain and texture and creamy yellow, as if formed of
condensed sunbeams. The sugar from which the common name is derived is, I think, the best of sweets. It
exudes from the heart-wood where wounds have been
made by forest fires or the ax, and forms irregular,
crisp, candy-like kernels of considerable size, something like clusters of resin beads. When fresh it is
white, but because most of the wounds on which it is
found have been made by fire the sap is stained and
the hardened sugar becomes brown. Indians are fond
of it, but on account of its laxative properties only
small quantities may be eaten. No tree lover will ever
forget his first meeting with the sugar pine. In most
pine trees there is the sameness of expression which
to most people is apt to become monotonous, for the
typical spiral form of conifers, however beautiful, af-
fords little scope for appreciable individual character.
The sugar pine is as free from conventionalities as
the most picturesque oaks. No two are alike, and
though they toss out their immense arms in what might

seem extravagant gestures they never lose their expression of serene majesty. They are the priests of pines and seem ever to be addressing the surrounding forest. The yellow pine is found growing with them on warm hillsides, and the silver fir on cool northern slopes; but, noble as these are, the sugar pine is easily king, and spreads his arms above them in blessing while they rock and wave in sign of recognition. The main branches are sometimes forty feet long, yet persistently simple, seldom dividing at all, excepting near the end; but anything like a bare cable appearance is prevented by the small, tasseled branchlets that extend all around them; and when these superb limbs sweep out symmetrically on all sides, a crown sixty or seventy feet wide is formed, which, gracefully poised on the summit of the noble shaft, is a glorious object. Commonly, however, there is a preponderance of limbs toward the east, away from the direction of the prevailing winds.

Although so unconventional when full-grown, the sugar pine is a remarkably proper tree in youth—a strict follower of coniferous fashions—slim, erect, with leafy branches kept exactly in place, each tapering in outline and terminating in a spiry point. The successive forms between the cautious neatness of youth and the bold freedom of maturity offer a delightful study. At the age of fifty or sixty years, the shy, fashionable form begins to be broken up. Specialized branches push out and bend with the great cones, giving individual character, that becomes more marked from year to year. Its most constant companion is the yellow pine. The Douglas spruce, libocedrus, sequoia, and the silver fir are also more or less associated with it; but on many deep-soiled mountain-sides, at an elevation of about 5000 feet above the sea, it forms the bulk of the forest, filling every swell and hollow and down-plunging ravine. The majestic crowns, approaching each other in bold curves, make a glorious canopy through which the tempered sunbeams pour, silvering the needles, and gilding the massive boles and the flowery, park-like ground into a scene of enchantment.

On the most sunny slopes the white-flowered, fragrant chamaebatia is spread like a carpet, brightened during early summer with the crimson sarcodes, the wild rose, and innumerable violets and gilias. Not even in the shadiest nooks will you find any rank, untidy weeds or unwholesome darkness. In the north sides of ridges the boles are more slender, and the ground is mostly occupied by an underbrush of hazel, ceanothus, and flowering dogwood, but not so densely as to prevent the traveler from sauntering where he will; while the crowning branches are never impenetrable to the rays of the sun, and never so interblended as to lose their individuality.

THE YELLOW OR SILVER PINE

The Silver Pine (*Pinus ponderosa*),[3] or Yellow Pine, as it is commonly called, ranks second among the pines of the Sierra as a lumber tree, and almost rivals the sugar pine in stature and nobleness of port. Because of its superior powers of enduring variations of climate and soil, it has a more extensive range than any other conifer growing on the Sierra. On the western slope it is first met at an elevation of about 2000 feet, and extends nearly to the upper limit of the timberline. Thence, crossing the range by the lowest passes, it descends to the eastern base, and pushes out for a considerable distance into the hot, volcanic plains, growing bravely upon well-watered moraines, gravelly

---

[3] *Ponderosa* is Western yellow pine. The term silver is applied in this part of the country to *Pinus monticola*.

lake basins, climbing old volcanoes and dropping ripe cones among ashes and cinders.

The average size of full-grown trees on the western slope, where it is associated with the sugar pine, is a little less than 200 feet in height and from five to six feet in diameter, though specimens considerably larger may easily be found. Where there is plenty of free sunshine and other conditions are favorable, it presents a striking contrast in form to the sugar pine, being a symmetrical spire, formed of a straight round trunk, clad with innumerable branches that are divided over and over again. Unlike the Yosemite form about one-half of the trunk is commonly branchless, but where it grows at all close three-fourths or more is naked, presenting then a more slender and elegant shaft than any other tree in the woods. The bark is mostly arranged in massive plates, some of them measuring four or five feet in length by eighteen inches in width, with a thickness of three or four inches, forming a quite marked and distinguishing feature. The needles are of a fine, warm, yellow-green color, six to eight inches long, firm and elastic, and crowded in handsome, radiant tassels on the upturning ends of the branches. The cones are about three or four inches long, and two and a half wide, growing in close, sessile clusters among the leaves.

The species attains its noblest form in filled-up lake basins, especially in those of the older yosemites, and as we have seen, so prominent a part does it form of their groves that it may well be called the Yosemite Pine.

The Jeffrey variety[4] attains its finest development in the northern portion of the range, in the wide basins of the McCloud and Pit Rivers, where it forms magnificent forests scarcely invaded by any other tree. It

[4] *Pinus Jeffreyi.*

differs from the ordinary form in size, being only about
half as tall, in its redder and more closely-furrowed
bark, grayish-green foliage, less divided branches, and
much larger cones; but intermediate forms come in
which make a clear separation impossible, although
some botanists regard it as a distinct species. It is this
variety of ponderosa that climbs storm-swept ridges
alone, and wanders out among the volcanoes of the
Great Basin. Whether exposed to extremes of heat or
cold, it is dwarfed like many other trees, and becomes
all knots and angles, wholly unlike the majestic forms
we have been sketching. Old specimens, bearing
cones about as big as pineapples, may sometimes be
found clinging to rifted rocks at an elevation of 7000
or 8000 feet, whose highest branches scarce reach
above one's shoulders.

I have often feasted on the beauty of these noble
trees when they were towering in all their winter grandeur, laden with snow—one mass of bloom; in summer,
too, when the brown, staminate clusters hang thick
among the shimmering needles, and the big purple
burrs are ripening in the mellow light; but it is during
cloudless wind-storms that these colossal pines are
most impressively beautiful. Then they bow like willows, their leaves streaming forward all in one direction, and, when the sun shines upon them at the required angle, entire groves glow as if every leaf were
burnished silver. The fall of tropic light on the crown
of a palm is a truly glorious spectacle, the fervid sun-
flood breaking upon the glossy leaves in long lance-
rays, like mountain water among boulders at the foot
of an enthusiastic cataract. But to me there is something more impressive in the fall of light upon these
noble, silver pine pillars: it is beaten to the finest dust
and shed off in myriads of minute sparkles that seem
to radiate from the very heart of the tree, as if like

rain, falling upon fertile soil, it had been absorbed to reappear in flowers of light. This species also gives forth the finest wind music. After listening to it in all kinds of winds, night and day, season after season, I think I could approximate to my position on the mountain by this pine music alone. If you would catch the tone of separate needles climb a tree in breezy weather. Every needle is carefully tempered and gives forth no uncertain sound, each standing out with no interference excepting during heavy gales; then you may detect the click of one needle upon another, readily distinguishable from the free wind-like hum.

When a sugar pine and one of this species equal in size are observed together, the latter is seen to be more simple in manners, more lively and graceful, and its beauty is of a kind more easily appreciated; on the other hand it is less dignified and original in demeanor. The yellow pine seems ever eager to shoot aloft, higher and higher. Even while it is drowsing in autumn sun-gold you may still detect a skyward aspiration, but the sugar pine seems too unconsciously noble and too complete in every way to leave room for even a heavenward care.

THE DOUGLAS SPRUCE

The Douglas Spruce (*Pseudotsuga Douglasii*)[5] is one of the largest and longest-lived of the giants that flourish throughout the main pine belt, often attaining a height of nearly 200 feet, and a diameter of six or seven feet. Where the growth is not too close, the stout, spreading branches, covering more than half of the trunk, are hung with innumerable slender, drooping sprays, handsomely feathered with the short leaves which radiate at right angles all around them. This vigorous tree is ever beautiful, welcoming the moun-

[5] Douglas fir, *Pseudotsuga taxifolia*.

tain winds and the snow as well as the mellow summer light; and it maintains its youthful freshness undiminished from century to century through a thousand storms. It makes its finest appearance during the months of June and July, when the brown buds at the ends of the sprays swell and open, revealing the young leaves, which at first are bright yellow, making the tree appear as if covered with gay blossoms; while the pendulous bracted cones, three or four inches long, with their shell-like scales, are a constant adornment.

The young trees usually are assembled in family groups, each sapling exquisitely symmetrical. The primary branches are whorled regularly around the axis, generally in fives, while each is draped with long, feathery sprays that descend in lines as free and as finely drawn as those of falling water.

In Oregon and Washington it forms immense forests, growing tall and mast-like to a height of 300 feet, and is greatly prized as a lumber tree. Here it is scattered among other trees, or forms small groves, seldom ascending higher than 5500 feet, and never making what would be called a forest. It is not particular in its choice of soil: wet or dry, smooth or rocky, it makes out to live well on them all. Two of the largest specimens, as we have seen, are in Yosemite; one of these, more than eight feet in diameter, is growing on a moraine; the other, nearly as large, on angular blocks of granite. No other tree in the Sierra seems so much at home on earthquake taluses and many of these huge boulder-slopes are almost exclusively occupied by it.

THE INCENSE CEDAR

Incense Cedar, (*Libocedrus decurrens*), already noticed among the Yosemite trees, is quite generally distributed throughout the pine belt without exclusively occupying any considerable area, or even making extensive groves. On the warmer mountain slopes it ascends to about 5000 feet, and reaches the climate most congenial to it at a height of about 4000 feet, growing vigorously at this elevation in all kinds of soil and, in particular, it is capable of enduring more moisture about its roots than any of its companions excepting only the sequoia.

Casting your eye over the general forest from some ridge-top you can identify it by the color alone of its spiry summits, a warm yellow-green. In its youth up to the age of seventy or eighty years, none of its companions forms so strictly tapered a cone from top to bottom. As it becomes older it oftentimes grows strikingly irregular and picturesque. Large branches push out at right angles to the trunk, forming stubborn elbows and shoot up parallel with the axis. Very old trees are usually dead at the top. The flat fragrant plumes are exceedingly beautiful: no waving fern-frond is finer in form and texture. In its prime the whole tree is thatched with them, but if you would see the libocedrus in all its glory you must go to the woods in midwinter when it is laden with myriads of yellow flowers about the size of wheat grains, forming a noble illustration of Nature's immortal virility and vigor. The mature cones, about three-fourths of an inch long, born on the ends of the plumy branchlets, serve to enrich still more the surpassing beauty of this winter-blooming tree-goldenrod.

THE SILVER FIRS

We come now to the most regularly planted and most clearly defined of the main forest belts, composed almost exclusively of two Silver Firs—*Abies concolor* and *Abies magnifica*—extending with but little interruption 450 miles at an elevation of from 5000 to 9000 feet above the sea. In its youth *A. concolor* is a

charmingly symmetrical tree with its flat plumy
branches arranged in regular whorls around the whit-
ish-gray axis which terminates in a stout, hopeful
shoot, pointing straight to the zenith, like an admonish-
ing finger. The leaves are arranged in two horizontal
rows along branchlets that commonly are less than
eight years old, forming handsome plumes, pinnated
like the fronds of ferns. The cones are grayish-green
when ripe, cylindrical, from three to four inches long,
and one and a half to two inches wide, and stand upright on the upper horizontal branches. Full-grown
trees in favorable situations are usually about 200 feet
high and five or six feet in diameter. As old age creeps
on, the rough bark becomes rougher and grayer, the
branches lose their exact regularity of form, many that
are snow-bent are broken off and the axis often becomes double or otherwise irregular from accidents to
the terminal bud or shoot. Nevertheless, throughout
all the vicissitudes of its three or four centuries of life,
come what may, the noble grandeur of this species,
however obscured, is never lost.

The magnificent Silver Fir, or California Red Fir
(*Abies magnifica*) is the most symmetrical of all the
Sierra giants, far surpassing its companion species in
this respect and easily distinguished from it by the
purplish-red bark, which is also more closely furrowed
than that of the white, and by its larger cones, its more
regularly whorled and fronded branches, and its
shorter leaves, which grow all around the branches
and point upward instead of being arranged in two
horizontal rows. The branches are mostly whorled in
fives, and stand out from the straight, red-purple bole
in level, or in old trees in drooping, collars, every
branch regularly pinnated like fern-fronds, making
broad plumes, singularly rich and sumptuous-looking.
The flowers are in their prime about the middle of

June; the male red, growing on the underside of the branches in crowded profusion, giving a very rich color to all the trees; the female greenish-yellow, tinged with pink, standing erect on the upper side of the topmost branches, while the tufts of young leaves, about as brightly colored as those of the Douglas spruce, make another grand show. The cones mature in a single season from the flowers. When mature they are about six to eight inches long, three or four in diameter, covered with a fine gray down and streaked and beaded with transparent balsam, very rich and precious-looking, and stand erect like casks on the topmost branches. The inside of the cone is, if possible, still more beautiful. The scales and bracts are tinged with red and the seed-wings are purple with bright iridescence. Both of the silver firs live between two and three centuries when the conditions about them are at all favorable. Some venerable patriarch may be seen heavily storm-marked, towering in severe majesty above the rising generation, with a protecting grove of hopeful saplings pressing close around his feet, each dressed with such loving care that not a leaf seems wanting. Other groups are made up of trees near the prime of life, nicely arranged as if Nature had culled them with discrimination from all the rest of the woods. It is from this tree, called Red Fir by the lumbermen, that mountaineers cut boughs to sleep on when they are so fortunate as to be within its limit. Two or three rows of the sumptuous plushy-fronded branches, overlapping along the middle, and a crescent of smaller plumes mixed to one's taste with ferns and flowers for a pillow, form the very best bed imaginable. The essence of the pressed leaves seems to fill every pore of one's body. Falling water makes a soothing hush, while the spaces between the grand spires afford noble openings through which to gaze dreamily into the starry sky.[6] The fir woods are fine sauntering-grounds at almost any time of the year, but finest in autumn when the noble trees are hushed in the hazy light and drip with balsam; and the flying, whirling seeds, escaping from the ripe cones, mottle the air like flocks of butterflies. Even in the richest part of these unrivaled forests where so many noble trees challenge admiration we linger fondly among the colossal firs and extol their beauty again and again, as if no other tree in the world could henceforth claim our love. It is in these woods the great granite domes arise that are so striking and characteristic a feature of the Sierra. Here, too, we find the best of the garden-meadows full of lilies. A dry spot a little way back from the margin of a silver fir lily-garden makes a glorious camp-ground, especially where the slope is toward the east with a view of the distant peaks along the summit of the range. The tall lilies are brought forward most impressively like visitors by the light of your campfire and the nearest of the trees with their whorled branches tower above you like larger lilies and the sky seen through the garden-opening seems one vast meadow of white lily stars.

THE TWO-LEAVED PINE

The Two-Leaved Pine (*Pinus contorta*, var. *Murrayana*),[7] above the Silver Fir zone, forms the bulk of the alpine forests up to a height of from 8000 to 9500 feet above the sea, growing in beautiful order on moraines scarcely changed as yet by post-glacial weathering. Compared with the giants of the lower regions this

---

[6] Cutting boughs is illegal in a National Park, and indefensible nowadays in the dry, slow-growing forests of the Sierra. Fortunately the air mattress and sleeping bag have been perfected, and the experience of sleeping beside falling water in the woods is as rewarding as ever.

[7] Lodgepole pine, *P. contorta*, var. Engelmann.

is a small tree, seldom exceeding a height of eighty or
ninety feet. The largest I ever measured was ninety
feet high and a little over six feet in diameter. The
average height of mature trees throughout the entire
belt is probably not far from fifty or sixty feet with
a diameter of two feet. It is a well-proportioned,
rather handsome tree with grayish-brown bark and
crooked, much-divided branches which cover the
greater part of the trunk, but not so densely as to prevent it being seen. The lower limbs, like those of most
other conifers that grow in snowy regions, curve downward, gradually take a horizontal position about half-
way up the trunk, then aspire more and more toward
the summit. The short, rigid needles in fascicles of two
are arranged in comparatively long cylindrical tassels
at the ends of the tough up-curving branches. The
cones are about two inches long, growing in clusters
among the needles without any striking effect except
while very young, when the flowers are of a vivid
crimson color and the whole tree appears to be dotted
with brilliant flowers. The staminate flowers are still
more showy on account of their great abundance, often
giving a reddish-yellow tinge to the whole mass of foliage and filling the air with pollen. No other pine on the
range is so regularly planted as this one, covering moraines that extend along the sides of the high rocky
valleys for miles without interruption. The thin bark
is streaked and sprinkled with resin as though it had
been showered upon the forest like rain.

Therefore this tree more than any other is subject
to destruction by fire. During strong winds extensive
forests are destroyed, the flames leaping from tree to
tree in continuous belts that go surging and racing onward above the bending wood like prairie-grass fires.
During the calm season of Indian summer the fire
creeps quietly along the ground, feeding on the

needles and cones; arriving at the foot of a tree, the
resiny bark is ignited and the heated air ascends in a
swift current, increasing in velocity and dragging the
flames upward. Then the leaves catch, forming an immense column of fire, beautifully spired on the edges
and tinted a rose-purple hue. It rushes aloft thirty or
forty feet above the top of the tree, forming a grand
spectacle, especially at night. It lasts, however, only a
few seconds, vanishing with magical rapidity, to be
succeeded by others along the fire-line at irregular intervals, tree after tree, up-flashing and darting, leaving
the trunks and branches scarcely scarred. The heat,
however, is sufficient to kill the tree and in a few years
the bark shrivels and falls off. Forests miles in extent
are thus killed and left standing, with the branches on,
but peeled and rigid, appearing gray in the distance
like misty clouds. Later the branches drop off, leaving
a forest of bleached spars. At length the roots decay
and the forlorn gray trunks are blown down during
some storm and piled one upon another, encumbering
the ground until, dry and seasoned, they are consumed
by another fire and leave the ground ready for a fresh
crop.

In sheltered lake-hollows, on beds of alluvium, this
pine varies so far from the common form that frequently it could be taken for a distinct species, growing in damp sods like grasses from forty to eighty feet
high, bending all together to the breeze and whirling
in eddying gusts more lively than any other tree in the
woods. I frequently found specimens fifty feet high
less than five inches in diameter. Being so slender and
at the same time clad with leafy boughs, it is often
bent and weighed down to the ground when laden
with soft snow; thus forming fine ornamental arches,
many of them to last until the melting of the snow in
the spring.

THE MOUNTAIN PINE

The Mountain Pine (*Pinus monticola*)[8] is the noblest tree of the alpine zone—hardy and long-lived,
towering grandly above its companions and becoming
stronger and more imposing just where other species
begin to crouch and disappear. At its best it is usually
about ninety feet high and five or six feet in diameter,
though you may find specimens here and there considerably larger than this. It is as massive and as suggestive of enduring strength as an oak. About two-
thirds of the trunk is commonly free of limbs, but
close, fringy tufts of spray occur nearly all the way
down to the ground. On trees that occupy exposed situations near its upper limit the bark is deep reddish-
brown and rather deeply furrowed, the main furrows
running nearly parallel to each other and connected on
the old trees by conspicuous cross-furrows. The cones
are from four to eight inches long, smooth, slender,
cylindrical and somewhat curved. They grow in clusters of from three to six or seven and become pendulous as they increase in weight. This species is nearly
related to the sugar pine and, though not half so tall,
it suggests its noble relative in the way that it extends
its long branches in general habit. It is first met on the
upper margin of the silver fir zone, singly, in what appears as chance situations without making much impression on the general forest. Continuing up through
the forests of the two-leaved pine it begins to show its
distinguishing characteristic in the most marked way
at an elevation of about 10,000 feet, extending its
tough, rather slender arms in the frosty air, welcoming
the storms and feeding on them and reaching sometimes to the grand old age of 1000 years.

[8] Western white pine.

THE WESTERN JUNIPER

The Juniper or Red Cedar (*Juniperus occidentalis*) is preëminently a rock tree, occupying the baldest domes and pavements in the upper silver fir and alpine zones, at a height of from 7000 to 9500 feet. In such situations, rooted in narrow cracks or fissures, where there is scarcely a handful of soil, it is frequently over eight feet in diameter and not much more in height. The tops of old trees are almost always dead, and large stubborn-looking limbs push out horizontally, most of them broken and dead at the end, but densely covered, and imbedded here and there with tufts or mounds of gray-green scale-like foliage. Some trees are mere storm-beaten stumps about as broad as long, decorated with a few leafy sprays, reminding one of the crumbling towers of old castles scantily draped with ivy. Its homes on bare, barren dome and ridge-top seem to have been chosen for safety against fire, for, on isolated mounds of sand and gravel free from grass and bushes on which fire could feed, it is often found growing tall and unscathed to a height of forty to sixty feet, with scarce a trace of the rocky angularity and broken limbs so characteristic a feature throughout the greater part of its range. It never makes anything like a forest; seldom even a grove. Usually it stands out separate and independent, clinging by slight joints to the rocks, living chiefly on snow and thin air and maintaining sound health on this diet for 2000 years or more. Every feature or every gesture it makes expresses steadfast, dogged endurance. The bark is of a bright cinnamon color and is handsomely braided and reticulated on thrifty trees, flaking off in thin, shining ribbons that are sometimes used by the Indians for tent matting. Its fine color and picturesqueness are appreciated by artists, but to me the juniper seems a singularly strange and taciturn tree. I have spent many a day and night in its company and always have found it silent and rigid. It seems to be a survivor of some ancient race, wholly unacquainted with its neighbors. Its broad stumpiness, of course, makes wind-waving or even shaking out of the question, but it is not this rocky rigidity that constitutes its silence. In calm, sun-days the sugar pine preaches like an enthusiastic apostle without moving a leaf. On level rocks the juniper dies standing and wastes insensibly out of existence like granite, the wind exerting about as little control over it, alive or dead, as it does over a glacier boulder.

I have spent a good deal of time trying to determine the age of these wonderful trees, but as all of the very old ones are honeycombed with dry rot I never was able to get a complete count of the largest. Some are undoubtedly more than 2000 years old, for though on deep moraine soil they grow about as fast as some of the pines, on bare pavements and smoothly glaciated, overswept ridges in the dome region they grow very slowly. One on the Starr King Ridge only two feet eleven inches in diameter was 1140 years old forty years ago. Another on the same ridge, only one foot seven and a half inches in diameter, had reached the age of 834 years. The first fifteen inches from the bark of a medium-size tree six feet in diameter, on the north Tenaya pavement, had 859 layers of wood. Beyond this the count was stopped by dry rot and scars. The largest I examined was thirty-three feet in girth, or nearly ten feet in diameter and, although I have failed to get anything like a complete count, I learned enough from this and many other specimens to convince me that most of the trees eight or ten feet thick, standing on pavements, are more than twenty centuries old rather than less. Barring accidents, for all I can see they would live forever; even when overthrown by

avalanches, they refuse to lie at rest, lean stubbornly
on their big branches as if anxious to rise, and while a
single root holds to the rock, put forth fresh leaves
with a grim, never-say-die expression.

THE MOUNTAIN HEMLOCK

As the juniper is the most stubborn and unshakeable
of trees in the Yosemite region, the Mountain Hemlock
(*Tsuga Mertensiana*) is the most graceful and pliant
and sensitive. Until it reaches a height of fifty or sixty
feet it is sumptuously clothed down to the ground
with drooping branches, which are divided again and
again into delicate waving sprays, grouped and arranged in ways that are indescribably beautiful, and
profusely adorned with small brown cones. The flowers
also are peculiarly beautiful and effective; the female
dark rich purple, the male blue, of so fine and pure a
tone that the best azure of the mountain sky seems to
be condensed in them. Though apparently the most
delicate and feminine of all the mountain trees, it grows
best where the snow lies deepest, at a height of from
9000 to 9500 feet, in hollows on the northern slopes of
mountains and ridges. But under all circumstances,
sheltered from heavy winds or in bleak exposure to
them, well fed or starved, even at its highest limit,
10,500 feet above the sea, on exposed ridge-tops where
it has to crouch and huddle close in low thickets, it still
contrives to put forth its sprays and branches in forms
of invincible beauty, while on moist, well-drained
moraines it displays a perfectly tropical luxuriance of
foliage, flowers and fruit. The snow of the first winter
storm is frequently soft, and lodges in the dense leafy
branches, weighing them down against the trunk, and
the slender, drooping axis, bending lower and lower
as the load increases, at length reaches the ground,

forming an ornamental arch. Then, as storm succeeds storm and snow is heaped on snow, the whole tree is at last buried, not again to see the light of day or move leaf or limb until set free by the spring thaws in June or July. Not only the young saplings are thus carefully covered and put to sleep in the whitest of white beds for five or six months of the year, but trees thirty feet high or more. From April to May, when the snow by repeated thawing and freezing is firmly compacted, you may ride over the prostrate groves without seeing a single branch or leaf of them. No other of our alpine conifers so finely veils its strength; poised in thin, white sunshine, clad with branches from head to foot, it towers in unassuming majesty, drooping as if unaffected with the aspiring tendencies of its race, loving the ground, conscious of heaven and joyously receptive of its blessings, reaching out its branches like sensitive tentacles, feeling the light and reveling in it. The largest specimen I ever found was nineteen feet seven inches in circumference. It was growing on the edge of Lake Hollow, north of Mount Hoffman, at an elevation of 9250 feet above the level of the sea, and was probably about a hundred feet in height. Fine groves of mature trees, ninety to a hundred feet in height, are growing near the base of Mount Conness. It is widely distributed from near the south extremity of the high Sierra northward along the Cascade Mountains of Oregon and Washington and the coast ranges of British Columbia to Alaska, where it was first discovered in 1827. Its northernmost limit, so far as I have observed, is in the icy fiords of Prince William Sound in latitude 61°, where it forms pure forests at the level of the sea, growing tall and majestic on the banks of glaciers. There, as in the Yosemite region, it is ineffably beautiful, the very loveliest of all the American conifers.

THE WHITEBARK PINE

The Dwarf Pine, or Whitebark Pine (*Pinus albicaulis*), forms the extreme edge of the timberline throughout nearly the whole extent of the range on both flanks. It is first met growing with the two-leaved pine on the upper margin of the alpine belt, as an erect tree from fifteen to thirty feet high and from one to two feet in diameter; thence it goes straggling up the flanks of the summit peaks, upon moraines or crumbling ledges, wherever it can get a foothold, to an elevation of from 10,000 to 12,000 feet, where it dwarfs to a mass of crumpled branches, covered with slender shoots, each tipped with a short, close-packed, leaf tassel. The bark is smooth and purplish, in some places almost white. The flowers are bright scarlet and rose-purple, giving a very flowery appearance little looked for in such a tree. The cones are about three inches long, an inch and a half in diameter, grow in rigid clusters, and are dark chocolate in color while young, and bear beautiful pearly-white seeds about the size of peas, most of which are eaten by chipmunks and the Clark's crows.[9] Pines are commonly regarded as sky-loving trees that must necessarily aspire or die. This species forms a marked exception, crouching and creeping in compliance with the most rigorous demands of climate; yet enduring bravely to a more advanced age than many of its lofty relatives in the sun-lands far below it. Seen from a distance it would never be taken for a tree of any kind. For example, on Cathedral Peak there is a scattered growth of this pine, creeping like mosses over the roof, nowhere giving hint of an ascending axis. While, approached quite near, it still appears matty and heathy, and one experiences no difficulty in walking over the

[9] Clark's nutcracker (*Nucifraga columbiana*).

top of it, yet it is seldom absolutely prostrate, usually attaining a height of three or four feet with a main trunk, and with branches outspread above it, as if in ascending they had been checked by a ceiling against which they had been compelled to spread horizontally. The winter snow *is* a sort of ceiling, lasting half the year; while the pressed surface is made yet smoother by violent winds armed with cutting sand-grains that bear down any shoot which offers to rise much above the general level, and that carve the dead trunks and branches in beautiful patterns.

During stormy nights I have often camped snugly beneath the interlacing arches of this little pine. The needles, which have accumulated for centuries, make fine beds, a fact well known to other mountaineers, such as deer and wild sheep, who paw out oval hollows and lie beneath the larger trees in safe and comfortable concealment. This lowly dwarf reaches a far greater age than would be guessed. A specimen that I examined, growing at an elevation of 10,700 feet, yet looked as though it might be plucked up by the roots, for it was only three and a half inches in diameter and its topmost tassel reached hardly three feet above the ground. Cutting it half through and counting the annual rings with the aid of a lens, I found its age to be no less than 255 years. Another specimen about the same height, with a trunk six inches in diameter, I found to be 426 years old, forty years ago; and one of its supple branchlets hardly an eighth of an inch in diameter inside the bark, was seventy-five years old, and so filled with oily balsam and seasoned by storms that I tied it in knots like a whip-cord.

THE NUT PINE

In going across the range from the Tuolumne River Soda Springs to Mono Lake one makes the acquaintance of the curious little Nut Pine, (*Pinus mono-phylla*). It dots the eastern flank of the Sierra to which it is mostly restricted in grayish bush-like patches, from the margin of the sage-plains to an elevation of from 7000 to 8000 feet. A more contented, fruitful and unaspiring conifer could not be conceived. All the species we have been sketching make departures more or less distant from the typical spire form, but none goes so far as this. Without any apparent cause it keeps near the ground, throwing out crooked, divergent branches like an orchard apple-tree, and seldom pushes a single shoot higher than fifteen or twenty feet above the ground.

The average thickness of the trunk is, perhaps, about ten or twelve inches. The leaves are mostly un-divided, like round awls, instead of being separated, like those of other pines, into twos and threes and fives. The cones are green while growing, and are usually found over all the tree, forming quite a marked feature as seen against the bluish-gray foliage. They are quite small, only about two inches in length, and seem to have but little space for seeds; but when we come to open them, we find that about half the entire bulk of the cone is made up of sweet, nutritious nuts, nearly as large as hazel-nuts. This is undoubtedly the most important food-tree on the Sierra, and furnishes the Mono, Carson, and Walker River Indians with more and better nuts than all the other species taken together. It is the Indian's own tree, and many a white man have they killed for cutting it down. Being so low, the cones are readily beaten off with poles, and the nuts procured by roasting them until the scales open. In bountiful seasons a single Indian may gather thirty or forty bushels.

VII

THE BIG TREES

Between the heavy pine and silver fir zones towers the Big Tree (*Sequoia gigantea*), the king of all the conifers in the world, "the noblest of the noble race." The groves nearest Yosemite Valley are about twenty miles to the westward and southward and are called the Tuolumne, Merced and Mariposa groves. It extends, a widely interrupted belt, from a very small grove on the middle fork of the American River to the head of Deer Creek, a distance of about 260 miles, its northern limit being near the thirty-ninth parallel, the southern a little below the thirty-sixth. The elevation of the belt above the sea varies from about 5000 to 8000 feet. From the American River to Kings River the species occurs only in small isolated groups so sparsely distributed along the belt that three of the gaps in it are from forty to sixty miles wide. But from Kings River southward the sequoia is not restricted to mere groves but extends across the wide rugged basins of the Kaweah and Tule Rivers in noble forests, a distance of nearly seventy miles, the continuity of this part of the belt being broken only by the main canyons. The Fresno, the largest of the northern groves, has an area of three or four square miles, a short distance to the southward of the famous Mariposa Grove. Along the south rim of the canyon of the south fork of Kings River there is a majestic sequoia forest about six miles long by two wide. This is the northernmost group that may fairly be called a forest.

Descending the divide between the Kings and Kaweah Rivers you come to the grand forests that form
the main continuous portion of the belt. Southward
the giants become more and more irrepressibly exuberant, heaving their massive crowns into the sky
from every ridge and slope, waving onward in graceful
compliance with the complicated topography of the
region. The finest of the Kaweah section of the belt is
on the broad ridge between Marble Creek and the
middle fork, and is called the Giant Forest. It extends
from the granite headlands, overlooking the hot San
Joaquin plains, to within a few miles of the cool glacial
fountains of the summit peaks. The extreme upper
limit of the belt is reached between the middle and
south forks of the Kaweah at a height of 8400 feet, but
the finest block of Big Tree forests in the entire belt is
on the north fork of Tule River, and is included in the
Sequoia National Park.

In the northern groves there are comparatively few
young trees or saplings. But here for every old storm-
beaten giant there are many in their prime and for
each of these a crowd of hopeful young trees and saplings, growing vigorously on moraines, rocky ledges,
along water courses and meadows. But though the
area occupied by the Big Tree increases so greatly
from north to south, there is no marked increase in the
size of the trees. The height of 275 feet or thereabouts
and a diameter of about twenty feet, four feet from
the ground is, perhaps, about the average size of what
may be called full-grown trees, where they are favorably located. The specimens twenty-five feet in diameter are not very rare and a few are nearly three hundred feet high. In the Calaveras Grove there are four
trees over 300 feet in height, the tallest of which as
measured by the Geological Survey is 325 feet. The
very largest that I have yet met in the course of my

explorations is a majestic old fire-scarred monument in
the Kings River forest. It is thirty-five feet and eight
inches in diameter inside the bark, four feet above
the ground. It is burned half through, and I spent a
day in clearing away the charred surface with a sharp
ax and counting the annual wood-rings with the aid of
a pocket lens. I succeeded in laying bare a section all
the way from the outside to the heart and counted a
little over four thousand rings, showing that this tree
was in its prime about twenty-seven feet in diameter
at the beginning of the Christian era. No other tree in
the world, as far as I know, has looked down on so
many centuries as the sequoia or opens so many impressive and suggestive views into history. Under the
most favorable conditions these giants probably live
5000 years or more, though few of even the larger trees
are half as old. The age of one that was felled in Calaveras Grove, for the sake of having its stump for a
dancing-floor, was about 1300 years, and its diameter
measured across the stump twenty-four feet inside the
bark. Another that was felled in the Kings River forest
was about the same size but nearly a thousand years
older (2200 years), though not a very old-looking
tree.[1]

So harmonious and finely balanced are even the
mightiest of these monarchs in all their proportions
that there is never anything overgrown or monstrous
about them. Seeing them for the first time you are
more impressed with their beauty than their size, their
grandeur being in great part invisible; but sooner or

[1] Scientists estimate the age of the oldest logged sequoia at
no more than 3200 years. Bristlecone pines (P. aristata) in the
White Mountains east of the Sierra Nevada are older. For size
and majesty, however, Sequoia gigantea has no rival. The Grizzly
Giant, in Mariposa Grove, probably the oldest tree in Yosemite,
is 209 feet high and has a base diameter of 34.7 feet. Specimens
in Giant Forest, Sequoia National Park, are even larger.

later it becomes manifest to the loving eye, stealing slowly on the senses like the grandeur of Niagara or of the Yosemite domes. When you approach them and walk around them you begin to wonder at their colossal size and try to measure them. They bulge considerably at the base, but not more than is required for beauty and safety and the only reason that this bulging seems in some cases excessive is that only a comparatively small section is seen in near views. One that I measured in the Kings River forest was twenty-five feet in diameter at the ground and ten feet in diameter 200 feet above the ground, showing the fineness of the taper of the trunk as a whole. No description can give anything like an adequate idea of their singular majesty, much less of their beauty. Except the sugar pine, most of their neighbors with pointed tops seem ever trying to go higher, while the Big Tree, soaring above them all, seems satisfied. Its grand domed head seems to be poised about as lightly as a cloud, giving no impression of seeking to rise higher. Only when it is young does it show like other conifers a heavenward yearning, sharply aspiring with a long quick-growing top. Indeed, the whole tree for the first century or two, or until it is one hundred or one hundred and fifty feet high, is arrowhead in form, and, compared with the solemn rigidity of age, seems as sensitive to the wind as a squirrel's tail. As it grows older, the lower branches are gradually dropped and the upper ones thinned out until comparatively few are left. These, however, are developed to a great size, divide again and again and terminate in bossy, rounded masses of leafy branchlets, while the head becomes dome-shaped, and is the first to feel the touch of the rosy beams of the morning, the last to bid the sun good night. Perfect specimens, unhurt by running fires or lightning, are singularly regular and symmetrical in general form, though not in the least conventionalized, for they show extraordinary variety in the unity and harmony of their general outline. The immensely strong, stately shafts are free of limbs for one hundred and fifty feet or so. The large limbs reach out with equal boldness in every direction, showing no weather side, and no other tree has foliage so densely massed, so finely molded in outline and so perfectly subordinate to an ideal type. A particularly knotty, angular, ungovernable-looking branch, from five to seven or eight feet in diameter and perhaps a thousand years old, may occasionally be seen pushing out from the trunk as if determined to break across the bounds of the regular curve, but like all the others it dissolves in bosses of branchlets and sprays as soon as the general outline is approached. Except in picturesque old age, after being struck by lightning or broken by thousands of snow-storms, the regularity of forms is one of their most distinguishing characteristics. Another is the simple beauty of the trunk and its great thickness as compared with its height and the width of the branches, which makes them look more like finely modeled and sculptured architectural columns than the stems of trees, while the great limbs look like rafters, supporting the magnificent dome-head. But though so consummately beautiful, the Big Tree always seems unfamiliar, with peculiar physiognomy, awfully solemn and earnest; yet with all its strangeness it impresses us as being more at home than any of its neighbors, holding the best right to the ground as the oldest, strongest inhabitant. One soon becomes acquainted with new species of pine and fir and spruce as with friendly people, shaking their outstretched branches like shaking hands and fondling their little ones, while the venerable aboriginal sequoia, ancient of other days, keeps you at a distance, looking as strange in aspect and behavior among its neighbor trees as would the mastodon among the homely bears and deer. Only the Sierra juniper is at all like it, standing rigid and unconquerable on glacier pavements for thousands of years, grim and silent, with an air of antiquity about as pronounced as that of the sequoia.

The bark of the largest trees is from one to two feet thick, rich cinnamon-brown, purplish on young trees, forming magnificent masses of color with the under-brush. Toward the end of winter the trees are in bloom, while the snow is still eight or ten feet deep. The female flowers are about three-eighths of an inch long, pale green, and grow in countless thousands on the ends of sprays. The male are still more abundant, pale yellow, a fourth of an inch long and when the pollen is ripe they color the whole tree and dust the air and the ground. The cones are bright grass-green in color, about two and a half inches long, one and a half wide, made up of thirty or forty strong, closely-packed, rhomboidal scales, with four to eight seeds at the base of each. The seeds are wonderfully small and light, being only from an eighth to a fourth of an inch long and wide, including a filmy surrounding wing, which causes them to glint and waver in falling and enables the wind to carry them considerable distances. Unless harvested by the squirrels, the cones discharge their seed and remain on the tree for many years. In fruitful seasons the trees are fairly laden. On two small branches one and a half and two inches in diameter I counted 480 cones. No other California conifer produces nearly so many seeds, except, perhaps, the other sequoia, the redwood of the Coast Mountains. Millions are ripened annually by a single tree, and in a fruitful year the product of one of the northern groves would be enough to plant all the mountain ranges in the world.

As soon as any accident happens to the crown, such as being smashed off by lightning, the branches beneath the wound, no matter how situated, seem to be excited, like a colony of bees that have lost their queen, and become anxious to repair the damage. Limbs that have grown outward for centuries at right angles to the trunk begin to turn upward to assist in making a new crown, each speedily assuming the special form of true summits. Even in the case of mere stumps, burned half through, some mere ornamental tuft will try to go aloft and do its best as a leader in forming a new head. Groups of two or three are often found standing close together, the seeds from which they sprang having probably grown on ground cleared for their reception by the fall of a large tree of a former generation. They are called "loving couples," "three graces," etc. When these trees are young they are seen to stand twenty or thirty feet apart, by the time they are full-grown their trunks will touch and crowd against each other and in some cases even appear as one.

It is generally believed that the sequoia was once far more widely distributed over the Sierra; but after long and careful study I have come to the conclusion that it never was, at least since the close of the glacial period, because a diligent search along the margins of the groves, and in the gaps between fails to reveal a single trace of its previous existence beyond its present bounds. Notwithstanding, I feel confident that if every sequoia in the range were to die today, numerous monuments of their existence would remain, of so imperishable a nature as to be available for the student more than ten thousand years hence.

In the first place, no species of coniferous tree in the range keeps its members so well together as the sequoia; a mile is, perhaps, the greatest distance of

any straggler from the main body, and all of those
stragglers that have come under my observation are
young, instead of old monumental trees, relics of a
more extended growth.

Again, the great trunks of the sequoia last for centuries after they fall. I have a specimen block of sequoia wood, cut from a fallen tree, which is hardly
distinguishable from a similar section cut from a living
tree, although the one cut from the fallen trunk has
certainly lain on the damp forest floor more than 380
years, probably thrice as long. The time-measure in
the case is simply this: When the ponderous trunk
to which the old vestige belonged fell, it sunk itself
into the ground, thus making a long, straight ditch,
and in the middle of this ditch a silver fir four feet
in diameter and 380 years old was growing, as I determined by cutting it half through and counting the
rings, thus demonstrating that the remnant of the
trunk that made the ditch has lain on the ground *more*
than 380 years. For it is evident that, to find the whole
time, we must add to the 380 years the time that the
vanished portion of the trunk lay in the ditch before
being burned out of the way, plus the time that passed
before the seed from which the monumental fir sprang
fell into the prepared soil and took root. Now, because
sequoia trunks are never wholly consumed in one
forest fire, and those fires recur only at considerable
intervals, and because sequoia ditches after being
cleared are often left unplanted for centuries, it becomes evident that the trunk-remnant in question may
probably have lain a thousand years or more. And
this instance is by no means a rare one.

Again, admitting that upon those areas supposed to
have been once covered with sequoia forests, every
tree may have fallen, and every trunk may have been
burned or buried, leaving not a remnant, many of the

ditches made by the fall of the ponderous trunks, and
the bowls made by their upturning roots, would remain patent for thousands of years after the last vestige of the trunks that made them had vanished. Much
of this ditch-writing would no doubt be quickly ef-
faced by the flood-action of overflowing streams and
rain-washing; but no inconsiderable portion would
remain enduringly engraved on ridge-tops beyond
such destructive action; for, where all the conditions
are favorable, it is almost imperishable. Now these
historic ditches and root-bowls occur in all the present
sequoia groves and forests, but, as far as I have observed, not the faintest vestige of one presents itself
outside of them.

We therefore conclude that the area covered by sequoia has not been diminished during the last eight
or ten thousand years, and probably not at all in post-
glacial time. Nevertheless, the questions may be
asked: Is the species verging toward extinction? What
are its relations to climate, soil, and associated trees?

All the phenomena bearing on these questions also
throw light, as we shall endeavor to show, upon the
peculiar distribution of the species, and sustain the
conclusion already arrived at as to the question of
former extension. In the northern groups, as we have
seen, there are few young trees or saplings growing up
around the old ones to perpetuate the race, and inasmuch as those aged sequoias, so nearly childless, are
the only ones commonly known, the species, to most
observers, seems doomed to speedy extinction, as being nothing more than an expiring remnant, van-
quished in the so-called struggle for life by pines and
firs that have driven it into its last strongholds in moist
glens where the climate is supposed to be excep-
tionally favorable. But the story told by the majestic
continuous forests of the south creates a very different

impression. No tree in the forest is more enduringly
established in concordance with both climate and soil.
It grows heartily everywhere—on moraines, rocky
ledges, along water-courses, and in the deep, moist
alluvium of meadows with, as we have seen, a multitude of seedlings and saplings crowding up around
the aged, abundantly able to maintain the forest in
prime vigor. So that if all the trees of any section of
the main sequoia forest were ranged together according to age, a very promising curve would be presented,
all the way up from last year's seedlings to giants, and
with the young and middle-aged portion of the curve
many times longer than the old portion. Even as far
north as the Fresno, I counted 536 saplings and seedlings, growing promisingly upon a landslip not exceeding two acres in area. This soil-bed was about seven
years old, and had been seeded almost simultaneously
by pines, firs, libocedrus, and sequoia, presenting a
simple and instructive illustration of the struggle for
life among the rival species; and it was interesting to
note that the conditions thus far affecting them have
enabled the young sequoias to gain a marked advantage. Toward the south where the sequoia becomes
most exuberant and numerous, the rival trees become
less so; and where they mix with sequoias they grow
up beneath them like slender grasses among stalks of
Indian corn. Upon a bed of sandy flood-soil I counted
ninety-four sequoias, from one to twelve feet high, on
a patch of ground once occupied by four large sugar
pines which lay crumbling beneath them—an instance
of conditions which have enabled sequoias to crowd
out the pines. I also noted eighty-six vigorous saplings
upon a piece of fresh ground prepared for their reception by fire. Thus fire, the great destroyer of the sequoia, also furnishes the bare ground required for its
growth from the seed. Fresh ground is, however, fur-

nished in sufficient quantities for the renewal of the forests without the aid of fire—by the fall of old trees. The soil is thus upturned and mellowed, and many trees are planted for every one that falls.

It is constantly asserted in a vague way that the Sierra was vastly wetter than now, and that the increasing drought will of itself extinguish the sequoia, leaving its ground to other trees supposed capable of flourishing in a drier climate. But that the sequoia can and does grow on as dry ground as any of its present rivals is manifest in a thousand places. "Why, then," it will be asked, "are sequoias always found only in well-watered places?" Simply because a growth of sequoias creates those streams. The thirsty mountaineer knows well that in every sequoia grove he will find running water, but it is a mistake to suppose that the water is the cause of the grove being there; on the contrary, the grove is the cause of the water being there. Drain off the water and the trees will remain, but cut off the trees, and the streams will vanish. Never was cause more completely mistaken for effect than in the case of these related phenomena of sequoia woods and perennial streams.

When attention is called to the method of sequoia stream-making, it will be apprehended at once. The roots of this immense tree fill the ground, forming a thick sponge that absorbs and holds back the rain and melting snow, only allowing it to ooze and flow gently. Indeed, every fallen leaf and rootlet, as well as long clasping root, and prostrate trunk, may be regarded as a dam hoarding the bounty of storm-clouds, and dispensing it as blessings all through the summer, instead of allowing it to go headlong in short-lived floods.

Since, then, it is a fact that thousands of sequoias are growing thriftily on what is termed dry ground, and even clinging like mountain pines to rifts in granite precipices, and since it has also been shown that the extra moisture found in connection with the denser growths is an effect of their presence, instead of a cause of their presence, then the notions as to the former extension of the species and its near approach to extinction, based upon its supposed dependence on greater moisture, are seen to be erroneous.

The decrease in the rain and snowfall since the close of the glacial period in the Sierra is much less than is commonly guessed. The highest post-glacial water-marks are well preserved in all the upper river channels, and they are not greatly higher than the spring flood-marks of the present; showing conclusively that no extraordinary decrease has taken place in the volume of the upper tributaries of post-glacial Sierra streams since they came into existence. But, in the meantime, eliminating all this complicated question of climatic change, the plain fact remains that the present rain and snowfall is abundantly sufficient for the luxuriant growth of sequoia forests. Indeed, all my observations tend to show that in a prolonged drought the sugar pines and firs would perish before the sequoia, not alone because of the greater longevity of individual trees, but because the species can endure more drought, and make the most of whatever moisture falls.

Again, if the restriction and irregular distribution of the species be interpreted as a result of the desiccation of the range, then instead of increasing as it does in individuals toward the south where the rainfall is less, it should diminish. If, then, the peculiar distribution of sequoia has not been governed by superior conditions of soil as to fertility or moisture, by what has it been governed?

In the course of my studies I observed that the northern groves, the only ones I was at first acquainted

JOSEPH N. LECONTE (1870-1950), who photographed all the pictures in this section except Plate 7, was a charter member and later president of the Sierra Club, and an enthusiastic explorer of the California mountains. He photographed these Yosemite scenes on 5 x 7 glass plates in the 1890s and early 1900s, when John Muir was writing his books. LeConte was a professor of mechanical engineering and hydraulic engineering at the University of California, Berkeley. He mapped and described the high country which is now the route of the John Muir Trail.

Ansel Adams has written that LeConte's hundreds of excellent photographs "are not the fruits of intellectual cogitations; they are the natural, inevitable selections of a man very much in tune with the world about him, very much aware of its beauty, and of the importance of accuracies and fluencies functioning together in expression.... [They] reveal a sensitive reaction to the finest moments of the mountain scene."

J. N. LeConte

PLATE 1. Merced River, Gates of the Valley. ...*the crystal Merced, River of Mercy, peacefully quiet, reflecting lilies and trees and the onlooking rocks....*

J. N. LeCont

PLATE 2. Wapama Fall and Rock Pool. ...here...Nature seems in
nowise moderate, for a short distance to the eastward...booms and
thunders the great Hetch Hetchy Fall, Wapama...

J. N. LeConte

PLATE 3. El Capitan from Old Big Oak Flat Road. ...*regarded by many as the most sublime feature of the Valley, is seen...standing... in most imposing grandeur, a type of permanence.*

PLATE 4. Yosemite Falls. *So grandly does this magnificent fall display itself from the floor of the Valley, few visitors take the trouble to climb the walls to gain nearer views....*

J. N. LeConte

PLATE 5. Lip of Upper Yosemite Fall. *This noble fall has far the richest, as well as the most powerful, voice of all the falls of the Valley....*

J. N. LeConte

PLATE 6. On the Crest of Lyell Glacier. The Lyell Glacier is about a mile wide and less than a mile long, but presents, nevertheless, all the essential characters of large, river-like glaciers:...

Philip Hyde

PLATE 7. Tenaya Lake, Mount Conness. The Indian name of Lake Tenaya is "Pyweak" – the lake of shining rocks.

J. N. LeConte

PLATE 8. Hetch Hetchy Valley. ... Hetch Hetchy Valley, far from being a plain, common rock-bound meadow, is a grand landscape garden, one of Nature's rarest and most precious mountain temples.

with, were located on just those portions of the general forest soil-belt that were first laid bare toward the close of the glacial period when the ice-sheet began to break up into individual glaciers. And while searching the wide basin of the San Joaquin, and trying to account for the absence of sequoia where every condition seemed favorable for its growth, it occurred to me that this remarkable gap in the sequoia belt fifty miles wide is located exactly in the basin of the vast, ancient *mer de glace* of the San Joaquin and Kings River basins which poured its frozen floods to the plain through this gap as its channel. I then perceived that the next great gap in the belt to the northward, forty miles wide, extending between the Calaveras and Tuolumne groves, occurs in the basin of the great ancient mer de glace of the Tuolumne and Stanislaus basins; and that the smaller gap between the Merced and Mariposa groves occurs in the basin of the smaller glacier of the Merced. The wider the ancient glacier, the wider the corresponding gap in the sequoia belt.

Finally, pursuing my investigations across the basins of the Kaweah and Tule, I discovered that the sequoia belt attained its greatest development just where, owing to the topographical peculiarities of the region, the ground had been best protected from the main ice-rivers that continued to pour past from the summit fountains long after the smaller local glaciers had been melted.

Taking now a general view of the belt, beginning at the south, we see that the majestic ancient glaciers were shed off right and left down the valleys of Kern and Kings rivers by the lofty protective spurs outspread embracingly above the warm sequoia-filled basins of the Kaweah and Tule. Then, next northward, occurs the wide sequoia-less channel, or basin of the ancient San Joaquin and Kings River mer de glace;

then the warm, protected spots of Fresno and Mariposa groves; then the sequoia-less channel of the ancient Merced glacier; next the warm, sheltered ground of the Merced and Tuolumne groves; then the sequoia-less channel of the grand ancient mer de glace of the Tuolumne and Stanislaus; then the warm old ground of the Calaveras and Stanislaus groves. It appears, therefore, that just where, at a certain period in the history of the Sierra, the glaciers were not, there the sequoia is, and just where the glaciers were, there the sequoia is not.

But although all the observed phenomena bearing on the post-glacial history of this colossal tree point to the conclusion that it never was more widely distributed on the Sierra since the close of the glacial epoch; that its present forests are scarcely past prime, if, indeed, they have reached prime; that the post-glacial day of the species is probably not half done; yet, when from a wider outlook the vast antiquity of the genus is considered, and its ancient richness in species and individuals,—comparing our Sierra Giant and *Sequoia sempervirens* of the Coast Range, the only other living species of sequoia,[2] with the twelve fossil species already discovered and described by Heer and Lesquereux, some of which flourished over vast areas in the Arctic regions and in Europe and our own territories, during tertiary and cretaceous times—then, indeed, it becomes plain that our two surviving species, restricted to narrow belts within the limits of California, are mere remnants of the genus, both as to species and individuals, and that they may be verging to extinction. But the verge of a period beginning in cretaceous times may have a breadth of tens of thousands of years, not to mention the possible

[2] In 1944 living examples of a closely related genus, *Metasequoia*, the Dawn Redwood, were discovered in central China.

existence of conditions calculated to multiply and re-
extend both species and individuals.

There is no absolute limit to the existence of any
tree. Death is due to accidents, not, as that of animals,
to the wearing out of organs. Only the leaves die of
old age. Their fall is foretold in their structure; but
the leaves are renewed every year, and so also are the
essential organs—wood, roots, bark, buds. Most of the
Sierra trees die of disease, insects, fungi, etc., but nothing hurts the Big Tree. I never saw one that was sick
or showed the slightest sign of decay. Barring accidents, it seems to be immortal. It is a curious fact
that all the very old sequoias had lost their heads by
lightning strokes. "All things come to him who waits."
But of all living things, sequoia is perhaps the only
one able to wait long enough to make sure of being
struck by lightning.

So far as I am able to see at present only fire and
the ax threaten the existence of these noblest of God's
trees. In Nature's keeping they are safe, but through
the agency of man destruction is making rapid progress, while in the work of protection only a good beginning has been made. The Fresno Grove, the Tuolumne, Merced and Mariposa groves are under the
protection of the Federal Government in the Yosemite
National Park. So are the General Grant and Sequoia
National Parks; the latter, established twenty-one
years ago, has an area of 240 square miles and is ef-
ficiently guarded by a troop of cavalry under the direction of the Secretary of the Interior; so also are the
small General Grant National Park, established at the
same time with an area of four square miles, and the
Mariposa Grove, about the same size and the small
Merced and Tuolumne group.[3] Perhaps more than

---

[3] The Fresno (Nelder) Grove is outside the Park, in Sierra
National Forest. Kings Canyon National Park, established in

half of all the Big Trees have been thoughtlessly sold
and are now in the hands of speculators and mill men.
It appears, therefore, that far the largest and important section of protected Big Trees is in the great Sequoia National Park, now easily accessible by rail to
Lemon Cove and thence by a good stage road into the
giant forest of the Kaweah and thence by trail to other
parts of the park; but large as it is it should be made
much larger. Its natural eastern boundary is the High
Sierra and the northern and southern boundaries are
the Kings and Kern Rivers. Thus could be included
the sublime scenery on the headwaters of these rivers
and perhaps nine-tenths of all the Big Trees in existence. All private claims within these bounds should
be gradually extinguished by purchase by the Government. The Big Tree, leaving all its higher uses out of
the count, is a tree of life to the dwellers of the plain
dependent on irrigation, a never-failing spring, sending living waters to the lowland. For every grove cut
down a stream is dried up. Therefore all California is
crying, "Save the trees of the fountains." Nor, judging
by the signs of the times, is it likely that the cry will
cease until the salvation of all that is left of *Sequoia
gigantea* is made sure.

1940, incorporates the former General Grant Park and is combined administratively with Sequoia National Park, forming a
preserve of 1309 square miles. Some Big Trees are unprotected
by park status, but much of Muir's purpose has been achieved.

VIII

THE FLOWERS

Yosemite was all one glorious flower garden before plows and scythes and trampling, biting horses came to make its wide open spaces look like farmers' pasture fields. Nevertheless, countless flowers still bloom every year in glorious profusion on the grand talus slopes, wall benches and tablets, and in all the fine, cool side-canyons up to the rim of the Valley, and beyond, higher and higher, to the summits of the peaks. Even on the open floor and in easily-reached side-nooks many common flowering plants have survived and still make a brave show in the spring and early summer. Among these we may mention tall œnotheras, *Pentstemon lutea*, and *P. Douglasii* with fine blue and red flowers; Spraguea, scarlet zauschneria, with its curious radiant rosettes characteristic of the sandy flats; mimulus, eunanus, blue and white violets, geranium, columbine, erythraea, larkspur, collomia, draperia, gilias, heleniums, bahia, goldenrods, daisies, honeysuckle; heuchera, bolandra, saxifrages, gentians;[1] in cool canyon nooks and on Clouds Rest and the base of Starr King Dome you may find *Primula suffrutescens*, the only wild primrose discovered in California, and the only known shrubby species in the genus. And there are several fine orchids, habenaria, and cypripedium,

[1] *Pentstemon lutea:* probably *P. laetus. P. Douglasii:* probably Pride of the Mountains, *P. Newberryi.* It is spraguea, *Calyptridium umbellatum,* which has curious radiant rosettes. Eunanus is a mimulus. Erythraea: now *Centaurium.* Bahia: now *Eriophyllum.*

the latter very rare, once common in the Valley near the foot of Glacier Point, and in a bog on the rim of the Valley near a place called Gentry's Station, now abandoned. It is a very beautiful species, the large oval lip white, delicately veined with purple; the other petals and the sepals purple, strap-shaped, and elegantly curled and twisted.

Of the lily family, fritillaria, smilacina, chlorogalum and several fine species of brodiæa, Ithuriel's spear, and others less prized are common, and the favorite calochortus, or Mariposa lily, a unique genus of many species, something like the tulips of Europe but far finer. Most of them grow on the warm foothills below the Valley, but two charming species, *C. cæruleus* and *C. nudus*,[2] dwell in springy places on the Wawona road a few miles beyond the brink of the walls.

The snow plant (*Sarcodes sanguinea*) is more admired by tourists than any other in California. It is red, fleshy and watery and looks like a gigantic asparagus shoot. Soon after the snow is off the ground it rises through the dead needles and humus in the pine and fir woods like a bright glowing pillar of fire. In a week or so it grows to a height of eight or twelve inches with a diameter of an inch and a half or two inches; then its long fringed bracts curl aside, allowing the twenty- or thirty-five-lobed, bell-shaped flowers to open and look straight out from the axis. It is said to grow up through the snow; on the contrary, it always waits until the ground is warm, though with other early flowers it is occasionally buried or half-buried for a day or two by spring storms. The entire plant—flowers, bracts, stem, scales, and roots—is fiery red. Its color should appeal to one's blood. Nevertheless, it is a singularly

[2] Neither of these is known to occur in Yosemite. The plant Muir calls *C. nudus* is *Calochortus minimus*, while the other is unknown, according to Carl Sharsmith.

cold and unsympathetic plant. Everybody admires it as a wonderful curiosity, but nobody loves it as lilies, violets, roses, daisies are loved. Without fragrance, it stands beneath the pines and firs lonely and silent, as if unacquainted with any other plant in the world; never moving in the wildest storms; rigid as if lifeless, though covered with beautiful rosy flowers.

Far the most delightful and fragrant of the Valley flowers is the Washington lily, white, moderate in size, with from three- to ten-flowered racemes. I found one specimen in the lower end of the Valley at the foot of the Wawona grade that was eight feet high, the raceme two feet long, with fifty-two flowers, fifteen of them open; the others had faded or were still in the bud. This famous lily is distributed over the sunny portions of the sugar-pine woods, never in large meadow-garden companies like the large and the small tiger lilies (*pardalinum* and *parvum*), but widely scattered, standing up to the waist in dense ceanothus and manzanita chaparral, waving its lovely flowers above the blooming wilderness of brush, and giving their fragrance to the breeze. It is now becoming scarce in the most accessible parts of its range on account of the high price paid for its bulbs by gardeners through whom it has been distributed far and wide over the flower-loving world. For, on account of its pure color and delicate, delightful fragrance, all lily lovers at once adopted it as a favorite.

The principal shrubs are manzanita and ceanothus, several species of each, azalea, *Rubus nutkanus*,[3] brier rose, choke-cherry, philadelphus, calycanthus, garrya, rhamnus, etc.

The manzanita never fails to attract particular attention. The species common in the Valley is usually about six or seven feet high, round-headed with in-

[3] Thimbleberry, *R. parviflorus*.

numerable branches, red or chocolate-color bark, pale
green leaves set on edge, and a rich profusion of small,
pink, narrow-throated, urn-shaped flowers, like those
of arbutus. The knotty, crooked, angular branches are
about as rigid as bones, and the red bark is so thin
and smooth on both trunk and branches, they look as
if they had been peeled and polished and painted. In
the spring large areas on the mountain up to a height
of eight or nine thousand feet are brightened with the
rosy flowers, and in autumn with their red fruit. The
pleasantly acid berries, about the size of peas, look like
little apples, and a hungry mountaineer is glad to eat
them, though half their bulk is made up of hard seeds.
Indians, bears, coyotes, foxes, birds and other mountain people live on them for weeks and months. The
different species of ceanothus usually associated with
manzanita are flowery fragrant and altogether delightful shrubs, growing in glorious abundance, not only in
the Valley, but high up in the forest on sunny or half-
shaded ground. In the sugar-pine woods the most
beautiful species is *C. integerrimus*, often called Cal-
ifornian lilac, or deer brush. It is five or six feet high
with slender branches, glossy foliage, and abundance
of blue flowers in close, showy panicles. Two species,
C. prostratus and *C. procumbens*,[4] spread smooth,
blue-flowered mats and rugs beneath the pines, and
offer fine beds to tired mountaineers. The commonest
species, *C. cordulatus*, is most common in the silver-fir
woods. It is white-flowered and thorny, and makes
dense thickets of tangled chaparral, difficult to wade
through or to walk over. But it is pressed flat every
winter by ten or fifteen feet of snow. The western
azalea makes glorious beds of bloom along the river
bank and meadows. In the Valley it is from two to
five feet high, has fine green leaves, mostly hidden be-

[4] *C. fresnensis* and *C. diversifolius*.

neath its rich profusion of large, fragrant white and
yellow flowers, which are in their prime in June, July
and August, according to the elevation, ranging from
3000 to 6000 feet. Near the azalea-bordered streams
the small wild rose,[5] resembling *R. blanda*, makes
large thickets deliciously fragrant, especially on a
dewy morning and after showers. Not far from these
azalea and rose gardens, *Rubus nutkanus*[6] covers the
ground with broad, soft, velvety leaves, and pure-
white flowers as large as those of its neighbor and
relative, the rose, and much finer in texture, followed
at the end of summer by soft red berries good for
everybody. This is the commonest and the most beautiful of the whole blessed, flowery, fruity *Rubus* genus.

There are a great many interesting ferns in the Valley and about it. Naturally enough the greater number
are rock ferns—pellæa, cheilanthes, polypodium, adiantum, woodsia, cryptogramma, etc., with small tufted
fronds, lining cool glens and fringing the seams of the
cliffs. The most important of the larger species are
woodwardia, aspidium, asplenium, and, above all, the
common pteris.[7] *Woodwardia radicans*[8] is a superb,
broad-shouldered fern five to eight feet high, growing
in vase-shaped clumps where the ground is nearly
level and on some of the benches of the north wall of
the Valley where it is watered by a broad trickling
stream. It thatches the sloping rocks, frond overlapping frond like roof shingles. The broad-fronded,
hardy *Pteris aquilina*,[9] the commonest of ferns, covers large areas on the floor of the Valley. No other fern

[5] Probably *R. gymnocarpa*, var. *pubescens*.

[6] *R. parviflorus*.

[7] Aspidium: California wood fern, *Dryopteris arguta*. Asplenium: Lady fern, *Athyrium filix-femina*. Common pteris: Bracken,
Pteridium aquilinum.

[8] Giant chain fern, *Woodwardia fimbriata*.

[9] Bracken, *Pteridium aquilinum*.

does so much for the color glory of autumn, with its
browns and reds and yellows, even after lying dead
beneath the snow all winter. It spreads a rich brown
mantle over the desolate ground in the spring before
the grass has sprouted, and at the first touch of sun-
heat its young fronds come rearing up full of faith and
hope through the midst of the last year's ruins.

Of the five species of pellæa, *P. Breweri* is the har-
diest as to enduring high altitudes and stormy weather
and at the same time it is the most fragile of the genus.
It grows in dense tufts in the clefts of storm-beaten
rocks, high up on the mountain-side on the very edge
of the fern line. It is a handsome little fern about four
or five inches high, has pale-green pinnate fronds, and
shining bronze-colored stalks about as brittle as glass.
Its companions on the lower part of its range are
Cryptogramma acrostichoides and *Phegopteris alpes-
tris*,[10] the latter with soft, delicate fronds, not in the
least like those of Rock fern, though it grows on the
rocks where the snow lies longest. *Pellaea Bridgesii*,
with blue-green, narrow, simply-pinnate fronds, is
about the same size as Breweri and ranks next to it as
a mountaineer, growing in fissures, wet or dry, and
around the edges of boulders that are resting on glacier
pavements with no fissures whatever. About a thousand feet lower we find the smaller, more abundant
P. densa[11] on ledges and boulder-strewn, fissured
pavements, watered until late in summer from oozing
currents, derived from lingering snowbanks. It is, or
rather was, extremely abundant between the foot of
the Nevada and the head of the Vernal Fall, but visitors with great industry have dug out almost every
root, so that now one has to scramble in out-of-the-way
places to find it. The three species of Cheilanthes in

[10] Alpine lady fern, *Athyrium alpestre,* var. *americanum.*
[11] Indian's Dream, *Cheilanthes siliquosa.*

the Valley—*C. californica, C. gracillima,* and *myrio-phylla,*[12] with beautiful two-to-four-pinnate fronds, an inch to five inches long, adorn the stupendous walls however dry and sheer. The exceedingly delicate *californica* is so rare that I have found it only once. The others are abundant and are sometimes accompanied by the little gold fern, *Gymnogramme triangularis,* and rarely by the curious little *Botrychium simplex,* some of them less than an inch high. The finest of all the rock ferns is *Adiantum pedatum,* lover of water-falls and the finest spray-dust. The homes it loves best are overleaning, cave-like hollows, beside the larger falls, where it can wet its fingers with their dewy spray. Many of these moss-lined chambers contain thousands of these delightful ferns, clinging to mossy walls by the slightest hold, reaching out their delicate finger-fronds on dark, shining stalks, sensitive and tremulous, throbbing in unison with every movement and tone of the falling water, moving each division of the frond separately at times, as if fingering the music.

May and June are the main bloom-months of the year. Both the flowers and falls are then at their best. By the first of August the midsummer glories of the Valley are past their prime. The young birds are then out of their nests. Most of the plants have gone to seed; berries are ripe; autumn tints begin to kindle and burn over meadow and grove, and a soft mellow haze in the morning sunbeams heralds the approach of Indian summer. The shallow river is now at rest, its flood-work done. It is now but little more than a series of pools united by trickling, whispering currents that steal softly over brown pebbles and sand with scarce an audible murmur. Each pool has a character of its own and, though they are nearly currentless, the

---

[12] *C. myriophylla* may be Bead fern, *C. covillei.*

night air and tree shadows keep them cool. Their
shores curve in and out in bay and promontory, giving
the appearance of miniature lakes, their banks in most
places embossed with brier and azalea, sedge and
grass and fern; and above these in their glory of autumn colors a mingled growth of alder, willow, dogwood and balm-of-Gilead;[13] mellow sunshine overhead, cool shadows beneath; light filtered and strained
in passing through the ripe leaves like that which
passes through colored windows. The surface of the
water is stirred, perhaps, by whirling water-beetles,
or some startled trout, seeking shelter beneath fallen
logs or roots. The falls, too, are quiet; no wind stirs,
and the whole Valley floor is a mosaic of greens and
purples, yellows and reds. Even the rocks seem
strangely soft and mellow, as if they, too, had ripened.

[13] Black cottonwood, *Populus trichocarpa.*

IX

THE BIRDS

The songs of the Yosemite winds and waterfalls are delightfully enriched with bird song, especially in the nesting time of spring and early summer. The most familiar and best known of all is the common robin, who may be seen every day, hopping about briskly on the meadows and uttering his cheery, enlivening call. The black-headed grosbeak, too, is here, with the Bullock oriole, and western tanager, brown song-sparrow, hermit thrush, the purple finch,—a fine singer, with head and throat of a rosy-red hue,—several species of warblers and vireos, kinglets, flycatchers, etc.

But the most wonderful singer of all the birds is the water-ouzel that dives into foaming rapids and feeds at the bottom, holding on in a wonderful way, living a charmed life.

Several species of humming-birds are always to be seen, darting and buzzing among the showy flowers. The little red-bellied nuthatches, the chickadees, and little brown creepers, thread the furrows of the bark of the pines, searching for food in the crevices. The large Steller's jay makes merry in the pine-tops; flocks of beautiful green swallows skim over the streams, and the noisy Clark's crow may oftentimes be seen on the highest points around the Valley; and in the deep woods beyond the walls you may frequently hear and see the dusky grouse and the pileated woodpecker, or woodcock almost as large as a pigeon. The junco or snow-bird builds its nest on the floor of the

Valley among the ferns; several species of sparrow are common and the beautiful lazuli bunting, a common bird in the underbrush, flitting about among the azalea and ceanothus bushes and enlivening the groves with his brilliant color; and on gravelly bars the spotted sandpiper is sometimes seen. Many woodpeckers dwell in the Valley; the familiar flicker, the Harris woodpecker and the species which so busily stores up acorns in the thick bark of the yellow pines.

The short, cold days of winter are also sweetened with the music and hopeful chatter of a considerable number of birds. No cheerier choir ever sang in snow. First and best of all is the water-ouzel, a dainty, dusky little bird about the size of a robin, that sings a sweet fluty song all winter and all summer, in storms and calms, sunshine and shadow, haunting the rapids and waterfalls with marvelous constancy, building his nest in the cleft of a rock bathed in spray. He is not webfooted, yet he dives fearlessly into foaming rapids, seeming to take the greater delight the more boisterous the stream, always as cheerful and calm as any linnet in a grove. All his gestures as he flits about amid the loud uproar of the falls bespeak the utmost simplicity and confidence—bird and stream one and inseparable. What a pair! yet they are well related. A finer bloom than the foam bell in an eddying pool is this little bird. We may miss the meaning of the loud-resounding torrent, but the flute-like voice of the bird —only love is in it.

A few robins, belated on their way down from the upper meadows, linger in the Valley and make out to spend the winter in comparative comfort, feeding on the mistletoe berries that grow on the oaks. In the depths of the great forests, on the high meadows, in the severest altitudes, they seem as much at home as in the fields and orchards about the busy habitations of man, ascending the Sierra as the snow melts, following the green footsteps of Spring, until in July or August the highest glacier meadows are reached on the summit of the Range. Then, after the short summer is over, and their work in cheering and sweetening these lofty wilds is done, they gradually make their way down again in accord with the weather, keeping below the snowstorms, lingering here and there to feed on huckleberries and frost-nipped wild cherries growing on the upper slopes. Thence down to the vineyards and orchards of the lowlands to spend the winter; entering the gardens of the great towns as well as parks and fields, where the blessed wanderers are too often slaughtered for food—surely a bad use to put so fine a musician to; better make stove wood of pianos to feed the kitchen fire.

The kingfisher winters in the Valley, and the flicker and, of course, the carpenter woodpecker, that lays up large stores of acorns in the bark of trees; wrens also, with a few brown and gray linnets, and flocks of the arctic bluebird, making lively pictures among the snow-laden mistletoe bushes. Flocks of pigeons are often seen, and about six species of ducks, as the river is never wholly frozen over. Among these are the mallard and the beautiful wood-duck, now less common on account of being so often shot at. Flocks of wandering geese used to visit the Valley in March and April, and perhaps do so still, driven down by hunger or stress of weather while on their way across the range. When pursued by the hunters I have frequently seen them try to fly over the walls of the Valley until tired out and compelled to re-alight. Yosemite magnitudes seem to be as deceptive to geese as to men, for after circling to a considerable height and forming regular harrow-shaped ranks they would suddenly find themselves in danger of being dashed against the face of the cliff, much nearer the bottom than the top. Then turning in confusion with loud screams they would try again and again until exhausted and compelled to descend. I have occasionally observed large flocks on their travels crossing the summits of the range at a height of 12,000 to 13,000 feet above the level of the sea, and even in so rare an atmosphere as this they seemed to be sustaining themselves without extra effort. Strong, however, as they are of wind and wing, they cannot fly over Yosemite walls, starting from the bottom.

A pair of golden eagles have lived in the Valley ever since I first visited it, hunting all winter along the northern cliffs and down the river canyon. Their nest is on a ledge of the cliff over which pours the Nevada Fall. Perched on the top of a dead spar, they were always interested observers of the geese when they were being shot at. I once noticed one of the geese compelled to leave the flock on account of being sorely wounded, although it still seemed to fly pretty well. Immediately the eagles pursued it and no doubt struck it down, although I did not see the result of the hunt. Anyhow, it flew past me up the Valley, closely pursued.

One wild, stormy winter morning after five feet of snow had fallen on the floor of the Valley and the flying flakes driven by a strong wind still thickened the air, making darkness like the approach of night, I sallied forth to see what I might learn and enjoy. It was impossible to go very far without the aid of snowshoes, but I found no great difficulty in making my way to a part of the river where one of my ouzels lived. I found him at home busy about his breakfast, apparently unaware of anything uncomfortable in the weather. Presently he flew out to a stone against which the icy current was beating, and turning his back to the wind, sang as delightfully as a lark in springtime.

After spending an hour or two with my favorite, I made my way across the Valley, boring and wallowing through the loose snow, to learn as much as possible about the way the other birds were spending their time. In winter one can always find them because they are then restricted to the north side of the Valley, especially the Indian Canyon groves, which from their peculiar exposure are the warmest.

I found most of the robins cowering on the lee side of the larger branches of the trees, where the snow could not fall on them, while two or three of the more venturesome were making desperate efforts to get at the mistletoe berries by clinging to the underside of the snow-crowned masses, back downward, something like woodpeckers. Every now and then some of the loose snow was dislodged and sifted down on the hungry birds, sending them screaming back to their companions in the grove, shivering and muttering like cold, hungry children.

Some of the sparrows were busy scratching and pecking at the feet of the larger trees where the snow had been shed off, gleaning seeds and benumbed insects, joined now and then by a robin weary of his unsuccessful efforts to get at the snow-covered mistletoe berries. The brave woodpeckers were clinging to the snowless sides of the larger boles and overarching branches of the camp trees, making short flights from side to side of the grove, pecking now and then at the acorns they had stored in the bark, and chattering aimlessly as if unable to keep still, evidently putting in the time in a very dull way. The hardy nuthatches were threading the open furrows of the barks in their usual industrious manner and uttering their quaint notes, giving no evidence of distress. The Steller's jays were, of course, making more noise and stir than all the other

birds combined; every coming and going with loud
bluster, screaming as if each had a lump of melting
sludge in his throat, and taking good care to improve
every opportunity afforded by the darkness and confusion of the storm to steal from the acorn stores of the
woodpeckers. One of the golden eagles made an impressive picture as he stood bolt upright on the top of
a tall pine-stump, braving the storm, with his back to
the wind and a tuft of snow piled on his broad shoulders, a monument of passive endurance. Thus every
storm-bound bird seemed more or less uncomfortable,
if not in distress. The storm was reflected in every gesture, and not one cheerful note, not to say song, came
from a single bill. Their cowering, joyless endurance
offered striking contrasts to the spontaneous, irrepres-
sible gladness of the ouzel, who could no more help
giving out sweet song than a rose sweet fragrance. He
must sing, though the heavens fall.

X

THE SOUTH DOME

With the exception of a few spires and pinnacles, the South Dome[1] is the only rock about the Valley that is strictly inaccessible without artificial means, and its inaccessibility is expressed in severe terms. Nevertheless many a mountaineer, gazing admiringly, tried hard to invent a way to the top of its noble crown —all in vain, until in the year 1875, George Anderson, an indomitable Scotchman, undertook the adventure. The side facing Tenaya Canyon is an absolutely vertical precipice from the summit to a depth of about 1600 feet, and on the opposite side it is nearly vertical for about as great a depth.[2] The southwest side presents a very steep and finely drawn curve from the top down a thousand feet or more, while on the northeast, where it is united with the Clouds Rest Ridge, one may easily reach a point called the Saddle, about seven hundred feet below the summit. From the Saddle the Dome rises in a graceful curve a few degrees too steep for unaided climbing, besides being de-

[1] Half Dome, which Muir also called by the Indian name Tissiack.

[2] Incredible climbing achievements have been made since Muir wrote. Whatever he might have thought of such "artificial means" as modern pitons, expansion bolts and nylon rope, he would have appreciated the daring of the young Sierra Club teams that ascended the vertical northwest face of Half Dome in 1958 and twice in 1960. The first ascent took five days of grueling effort and exposure, the others three days and two days respectively.

fended by overleaning ends of the concentric dome layers of the granite.

A year or two before Anderson gained the summit, John Conway, the master trail-builder of the Valley, and his little sons, who climbed smooth rocks like lizards, made a bold effort to reach the top by climbing barefooted up the grand curve with a rope which they fastened at irregular intervals by means of eye-bolts driven into joints of the rock. But finding that the upper part would require laborious drilling, they abandoned the attempt, glad to escape from the dangerous position they had reached, some 300 feet above the Saddle. Anderson began with Conway's old rope, which had been left in place, and resolutely drilled his way to the top, inserting eye-bolts five to six feet apart, and making his rope fast to each in succession, resting his feet on the last bolt while he drilled a hole for the next above. Occasionally some irregularity in the curve, or slight foothold, would enable him to climb a few feet without a rope, which he would pass and begin drilling again, and thus the whole work was accomplished in a few days. From this slender beginning he proposed to construct a substantial stairway which he hoped to complete in time for the next year's travel, but while busy getting out timber for his stairway and dreaming of the wealth he hoped to gain from tolls, he was taken sick and died all alone in his little cabin.

On the 10th of November, after returning from a visit to Mount Shasta, a month or two after Anderson had gained the summit, I made haste to the Dome, not only for the pleasure of climbing, but to see what I might learn. The first winter storm-clouds had blossomed and the mountains and all the high points about the Valley were mantled in fresh snow. I was, therefore, a little apprehensive of danger from the slipperi-

ness of the rope and the rock. Anderson himself tried
to prevent me from making the attempt, refusing to
believe that anyone could climb his rope in the snow-
muffled condition in which it then was. Moreover, the
sky was overcast and solemn snow-clouds began to
curl around the summit, and my late experiences on
icy Shasta came to mind. But reflecting that I had
matches in my pocket, and that a little fire-wood
might be found, I concluded that in case of a storm
the night could be spent on the Dome without suf-
fering anything worth minding, no matter what the
clouds might bring forth. I therefore pushed on and
gained the top.

It was one of those brooding, changeful days that
come between the Indian summer and winter, when
the leaf colors have grown dim and the clouds come
and go among the cliffs like living creatures looking for
work: now hovering aloft, now caressing rugged rock-
brows with great gentleness, or, wandering afar over
the tops of the forests, touching the spires of fir and
pine with their soft silken fringes as if trying to tell
the glad news of the coming of snow.

The first view was perfectly glorious. A massive
cloud of pure pearl luster, apparently as fixed and
calm as the meadows and groves in the shadow beneath it, was arched across the Valley from wall to
wall, one end resting on the grand abutment of El
Capitan, the other on Cathedral Rocks. A little later, as
I stood on the tremendous verge overlooking Mirror
Lake, a flock of smaller clouds, white as snow, came
from the north, trailing their downy skirts over the
dark forests, and entered the Valley with solemn god-
like gestures through Indian Canyon and over the
North Dome and Royal Arches, moving swiftly, yet
with majestic deliberation. On they came, nearer and
nearer, gathering and massing beneath my feet and

filling the Tenaya Canyon. Then the sun shone free,
lighting the pearly gray surface of the cloud-like sea
and making it glow. Gazing, admiring, I was startled to
see for the first time the rare optical phenomenon of
the "Specter of the Brocken." My shadow, clearly out-
lined, about half a mile long, lay upon this glorious
white surface with startling effect. I walked back and
forth, waved my arms and struck all sorts of attitudes,
to see every slightest movement enormously exagger-
ated. Considering that I have looked down so many
times from mountain tops on seas of all sorts of clouds,
it seems strange that I should have seen the "Brocken
Specter" only this once. A grander surface and a
grander standpoint, however, could hardly have been
found in all the Sierra.

After this grand show the cloud-sea rose higher,
wreathing the Dome, and for a short time submerging
it, making darkness like night, and I began to think
of looking for a camp-ground in a cluster of dwarf
pines. But soon the sun shone free again, the clouds,
sinking lower and lower, gradually vanished, leaving
the Valley with its Indian-summer colors apparently
refreshed, while to the eastward the summit-peaks,
clad in new snow, towered along the horizon in glorious array.

Though apparently it is perfectly bald, there are
four clumps of pines growing on the summit, repre-
senting three species, *Pinus albicaulis*, *P. contorta* and
P. ponderosa, var. *Jeffreyi*—all three, of course, re-
pressed and storm-beaten. The alpine spiræa grows
here also and blossoms profusely with potentilla, erig-
eron, eriogonum, pentstemon, solidago, and an interesting species of onion, and four or five species of
grasses and sedges. None of these differs in any respect
from those of other summits of the same height,

excepting the curious little narrow-leaved, waxen-bulbed onion,[3] which I had not seen elsewhere.

Notwithstanding the enthusiastic eagerness of tourists to reach the crown of the Dome the views of the Valley from this lofty standpoint are less striking than from many other points comparatively low, chiefly on account of the foreshortening effect produced by looking down from so great a height. The North Dome is dwarfed almost beyond recognition, the grand sculpture of the Royal Arches is scarcely noticeable, and the whole range of walls on both sides seem comparatively low, especially when the Valley is flooded with noon sunshine; while the Dome itself, the most sublime feature of all the Yosemite views, is out of sight beneath one's feet. The view of Little Yosemite Valley is very fine, though inferior to one obtained from the base of the Starr King cone, but the summit landscapes towards Mounts Ritter, Lyell, Dana, Conness, and the Merced Group, are very effective and complete.

No one has attempted to carry out Anderson's plan of making the Dome accessible.[4] For my part I should prefer leaving it in pure wildness, though, after all, no great damage could be done by tramping over it. The surface would be strewn with tin cans and bottles, but the winter gales would blow the rubbish away. Avalanches might strip off any sort of stairway or ladder that might be built. Blue jays and Clark's crows have trodden the Dome for many a day, and so have beetles and chipmunks, and Tissiack would hardly be more "conquered" or spoiled should man be added to her list

[3] Either *Allium tribracteatum* or *A. obtusum.*

[4] Since 1919 there have been fixed cables to provide handrails for the hundreds who ascend the Dome each year. Wooden footrests are placed at ten-foot intervals. Despite the exposure, no special skill is required. Rubber-soled shoes are essential.

of visitors. His louder scream and heavier scrambling would not stir a line of her countenance.

When the sublime ice-floods of the glacial period poured down the flank of the range over what is now Yosemite Valley, they were compelled to break through a dam of domes extending across from Mount Starr King to North Dome; and as the period began to draw near a close the shallowing ice-currents were divided and the South Dome was, perhaps, the first to emerge, burnished and shining like a mirror above the surface of the icy sea; and though it has sustained the wear and tear of the elements tens of thousands of years, it yet remains a telling monument of the action of the great glaciers that brought it to light. Its entire surface is still covered with glacial hieroglyphics whose interpretation is the reward of all who devoutly study them.[5]

[5] It is now believed that Half Dome was not glaciated above the 8100 foot level.

XI

THE ANCIENT YOSEMITE GLACIERS: HOW THE VALLEY WAS FORMED

All California has been glaciated, the low plains and valleys as well as the mountains.[1] Traces of an ice-sheet, thousands of feet in thickness, beneath whose heavy folds the present landscapes have been molded, may be found everywhere, though glaciers now exist only among the peaks of the High Sierra. No other mountain chain on this or any other of the continents that I have seen is so rich as the Sierra in bold, striking, well-preserved glacial monuments. Indeed, every feature is more or less tellingly glacial. Not a peak, ridge, dome, canyon, yosemite, lake-basin, stream or forest will you see that does not in some way explain the past existence and modes of action of flowing, grinding, sculpturing, soil-making, scenery-making ice. For, notwithstanding the post-glacial agents—the air, rain, snow, frost, river, avalanche, etc.—have been at work upon the greater portion of the range for tens of thousands of stormy years, each engraving its own characters more and more deeply over those of the ice, the latter are so enduring and so heavily emphasized, they still rise in sublime relief, clear and legible, through every after-inscription. The landscapes of North Greenland, Antarctica, and some of those of our

[1] Definitive studies, including the work of François E. Matthes, indicate that the glacial mantle was confined wholly to the upper parts of the Sierra and did not approach the western base of the range.

own Alaska, are still being fashioned beneath a slow-crawling mantle of ice, from a quarter of a mile to probably more than a mile in thickness, presenting noble illustrations of the ancient condition of California, when its sublime scenery lay hidden in process of formation. On the Himalaya, the mountains of Norway and Switzerland, the Caucasus, and on most of those of Alaska, their ice-mantle has been melted down into separate glaciers that flow river-like through the valleys, illustrating a similar past condition in the Sierra, when every canyon and valley was the channel of an ice-stream, all of which may be easily traced back to their fountains, where some sixty-five or seventy of their topmost residual branches still linger beneath protecting mountain shadows.

The change from one to another of those glacial conditions was slow as we count time. When the great cycle of snow years, called the Glacial Period, was nearly complete in California, the ice-mantle, wasting from season to season faster than it was renewed, began to withdraw from the lowlands and gradually became shallower everywhere. Then the highest of the Sierra domes and dividing ridges, containing distinct glaciers between them, began to appear above the icy sea. These first river-like glaciers remained united in one continuous sheet toward the summit of the range for many centuries. But as the snowfall diminished, and the climate became milder, this upper part of the ice-sheet was also in turn separated into smaller distinct glaciers, and these again into still smaller ones, while at the same time all were growing shorter and shallower, though fluctuations of the climate now and then occurred that brought their receding ends to a standstill, or even enabled them to advance for a few tens or hundreds of years.

Meanwhile, hardy, home-seeking plants and animals, after long waiting, flocked to their appointed places, pushing bravely on higher and higher, along every sun-warmed slope, closely following the retreating ice, which, like shreds of summer clouds, at length vanished from the new-born mountains, leaving them in all their main, telling features nearly as we find them now.

Tracing the ways of glaciers, learning how Nature sculptures mountain-waves in making scenery-beauty that so mysteriously influences every human being, is glorious work.

The most striking and attractive of the glacial phenomena in the upper Yosemite region are the polished glacier pavements, because they are so beautiful, and their beauty is of so rare a kind, so unlike any portion of the loose, deeply weathered lowlands where people make homes and earn their bread. They are simply flat or gently undulating areas of hard resisting granite, which present the unchanged surface upon which with enormous pressure the ancient glaciers flowed. They are found in most perfect condition in the subalpine region, at an elevation of from eight thousand to nine thousand feet. Some are miles in extent, only slightly interrupted by spots that have given way to the weather, while the best preserved portions reflect the sunbeams like calm water or glass, and shine as if polished afresh every day, notwithstanding they have been exposed to corroding rains, dew, frost, and snow measureless thousands of years.

The attention of wandering hunters and prospectors, who see so many mountain wonders, is seldom commanded by other glacial phenomena, moraines however regular and artificial-looking, canyons however deep or strangely modeled, rocks however high; but when they come to these shining pavements they stop and stare in wondering admiration, kneel again and again to examine the brightest spots, and try hard to account for their mysterious shining smoothness. They may have seen the winter avalanches of snow descending in awful majesty through the woods, scouring the rocks and sweeping away like weeds the trees that stood in their way, but conclude that this cannot be the work of avalanches, because the scratches and fine polished striæ show that the agent, whatever it was, moved along the sides of high rocks and ridges and up over the tops of them as well as down their slopes. Neither can they see how water may possibly have been the agent, for they find the same strange polish upon ridges and domes thousands of feet above the reach of any conceivable flood. Of all the agents of whose work they know anything, only the wind seems capable of moving across the face of the country in the directions indicated by the scratches and grooves. The Indian name of Lake Tenaya is "Pyweak"—the lake of shining rocks. One of the Yosemite tribe, Indian Tom, came to me and asked if I could tell him what had made the Tenaya rocks so smooth.[2] Even dogs and horses, when first led up the mountains, study geology to this extent that they gaze wonderingly at the strange brightness of the ground and smell it, and place their feet cautiously upon it as if afraid of falling or sinking.

In the production of this admirable hard finish, the glaciers in many places flowed with a pressure of more than a thousand tons to the square yard, planing down granite, slate, and quartz alike, and bringing out the veins and crystals of the rocks with beautiful distinctness. Over large areas below the sources of the Tuol-

[2] Glacier-marked granite is seen throughout the Lake Tenaya area, but one of the points of dispute during realignment of the Tioga Road (completed 1961) was the blasting to bits of some of the finest accessible specimens of glacial striation and polish.

umne and Merced the granite is porphyritic; feldspar crystals an inch or two in length in many places form the greater part of the rock, and these, when planed off level with the general surface, give rise to a beautiful mosaic on which the happy sunbeams plash and glow in passionate enthusiasm. Here lie the brightest of all the Sierra landscapes. The range both to the north and south of this region was, perhaps, glaciated about as heavily, but because the rocks are less resisting, their polished surfaces have mostly given way to the weather, leaving only small imperfect patches. The lowest remnants of the old glacial surface occur at an elevation of from 3000 to 5000 feet above the sea-level, and twenty to thirty miles below the axis of the range. The short, steeply inclined canyons of the eastern flank also contain enduring, brilliantly striated and polished rocks, but these are less magnificent than those of the broad western flank.

One of the best general views of the brightest and best of the Yosemite park landscapes that every Yosemite tourist should see, is to be had from the top of Fairview Dome, a lofty conoidal rock near Cathedral Peak that long ago I named the Tuolumne Glacier Monument, one of the most striking and best preserved of the domes. Its burnished crown is about 1500 feet above the Tuolumne Meadows and 10,000 above the sea. At first sight it seems inaccessible, though a good climber will find it may be scaled on the south side. About half-way up you will find it so steep that there is danger of slipping, but feldspar crystals, two or three inches long, of which the rock is full, having offered greater resistance to atmospheric erosion than the mass of the rock in which they are imbedded, have been brought into slight relief in some places, roughening the surface here and there, and affording helping footholds.

The summit is burnished and scored like the sides and base, the scratches and striæ indicating that the mighty Tuolumne Glacier swept over it as if it were only a mere boulder in the bottom of its channel. The pressure it withstood must have been enormous. Had it been less solidly built it would have been carried away, ground into moraine fragments, like the adjacent rock in which it lay imbedded; for, great as it is, it is only a hard residual knot like the Yosemite domes, brought into relief by the removal of less resisting rock about it; an illustration of the survival of the strongest and most favorably situated.

Hardly less wonderful is the resistance it has offered to the trying mountain weather since first its crown rose above the icy sea. The whole quantity of post-glacial wear and tear it has suffered has not degraded it a hundredth of an inch, as may readily be shown by the polished portions of the surface. A few erratic boulders, nicely poised on its crown, tell an interesting story. They came from the summit-peaks twelve miles away, drifting like chips on the frozen sea, and were stranded here when the top of the Monument merged from the ice, while their companions, whose positions chanced to be above the slopes of the sides where they could not find rest, were carried farther on by falling back on the shallowing ice current.

The general view from the summit consists of a sublime assemblage of ice-born rocks and mountains, long wavering ridges, meadows, lakes, and forest-covered moraines, hundreds of square miles of them. The lofty summit-peaks rise grandly along the sky to the east, the gray pillared slopes of the Hoffman Range toward the west, and a billowy sea of shining rocks like the Monument, some of them almost as high and which from their peculiar sculpture seem to be rolling westward in the middle ground, something like breaking waves. Immediately beneath you are the Big Tuolumne Meadows, smooth lawns with large breadths of woods on either side, and watered by the young Tuolumne River, rushing cool and clear from its many snow- and ice-fountains. Nearly all the upper part of the basin of the Tuolumne Glacier is in sight, one of the greatest and most influential of all the Sierra ice-rivers. Lavishly flooded by many a noble affluent from the ice-laden flanks of Mounts Dana, Lyell, McClure, Gibbs, Conness, it poured its majestic outflowing current full against the end of the Hoffman Range, which divided and deflected it to right and left, just as a river of water is divided against an island in the middle of its channel. Two distinct glaciers were thus formed, one of which flowed through the great Tuolumne Canyon and Hetch Hetchy Valley, while the other swept upward in a deep current two miles wide across the divide, five hundred feet high between the basins of the Tuolumne and Merced, into the Tenaya Basin, and thence down through the Tenaya Canyon and Yosemite.

The map-like distinctness and freshness of this glacial landscape cannot fail to excite the attention of every beholder, no matter how little of its scientific significance may be recognized. These bald, westward-leaning rocks, with their rounded backs and shoulders toward the glacier fountains of the summit-mountains, and their split, angular fronts looking in the opposite direction, explain the tremendous grinding force with which the ice-flood passed over them, and also the direction of its flow. And the mountain peaks around the sides of the upper general Tuolumne Basin, with their sharp unglaciated summits and polished rounded sides, indicate the height to which the glaciers rose; while the numerous moraines, curving and swaying in beautiful lines, mark the boundaries of the main trunk

and its tributaries as they existed toward the close of
the glacial winter. None of the commercial highways
of the land or sea, marked with buoys and lamps,
fences, and guide-boards, is so unmistakably indicated
as are these broad, shining trails of the vanished Tuolumne Glacier and its far-reaching tributaries.

I should like now to offer some nearer views of a
few characteristic specimens of these wonderful old
ice-streams, though it is not easy to make a selection
from so vast a system intimately interblended. The
main branches of the Merced Glacier are, perhaps,
best suited to our purpose, because their basins, full of
telling inscriptions, are the ones most attractive and accessible to the Yosemite visitors who like to look beyond the Valley walls. They number five, and may well
be called Yosemite glaciers, since they were the agents
Nature used in developing and fashioning the grand
Valley. The names I have given them are, beginning
with the northernmost, Yosemite Creek, Hoffman,
Tenaya, South Lyell, and Illilouette Glaciers. These
all converged in admirable poise around from northeast to southeast, welded themselves together into the
main Yosemite Glacier, which, grinding gradually
deeper, swept down through the Valley, receiving
small tributaries on its way from the Indian, Sentinel,
and Pohono Canyons; and at length flowed out of the
Valley, and on down the range in a general westerly
direction. At the time that the tributaries mentioned
above were well defined as to their boundaries, the
upper portion of the Valley walls, and the highest rocks
about them, such as the domes, the uppermost of the
Three Brothers and the Sentinel, rose above the surface of the ice. But during the Valley's earlier history,
all its rocks, however lofty, were buried beneath a continuous sheet, which swept on above and about them
like the wind, the upper portion of the current flowing

steadily, while the lower portion went mazing and swedging down in the crooked and dome-blocked canyons toward the head of the Valley.[3]

Every glacier of the Sierra fluctuated in width and depth and length, and consequently in degree of individuality, down to the latest glacial days. It must, therefore, be borne in mind that the following description of the Yosemite glaciers applies only to their separate condition, and to that phase of their separate condition that they presented toward the close of the glacial period after most of their work was finished, and all the more telling features of the Valley and the adjacent region were brought into relief.

The comparatively level, many-fountained Yosemite Creek Glacier was about fourteen miles in length by four or five in width, and from five hundred to a thousand feet deep. Its principal tributaries, drawing their sources from the northern spurs of the Hoffman Range, at first pursued a westerly course; then, uniting with each other, and a series of short affluents from the western rim of the basin, the trunk thus formed swept around to the southward in a magnificent curve, and poured its ice over the north wall of Yosemite in cascades about two miles wide. This broad and comparatively shallow glacier formed a sort of crawling, wrinkled ice-cloud, that gradually became more regular in shape and river-like as it grew older. Encircling peaks began to overshadow its highest fountains, rock islets rose here and there amid its ebbing currents, and its picturesque banks, adorned with domes and round-backed ridges, extended in massive grandeur down to the brink of the Yosemite walls.

In the meantime the chief Hoffman tributaries, slowly receding to the shelter of the shadows covering

[3] Maps of the Yosemite glaciers by Matthes show that several of the peaks above the rim of the Valley were not glaciated.

their fountains, continued to live and work independently, spreading soil, deepening lake-basins and giving finishing touches to the sculpture in general. At length these also vanished, and the whole basin is now full of light. Forests flourish luxuriantly upon its ample moraines, lakes and meadows shine and bloom amid its polished domes, and a thousand gardens adorn the banks of its streams.

It is to the great width and even slope of the Yosemite Creek Glacier that we owe the unrivaled height and sheerness of the Yosemite Falls. For had the positions of the ice-fountains and the structure of the rocks been such as to cause down-thrusting concentration of the Glacier as it approached the Valley, then, instead of a high vertical fall we should have had a long slanting cascade, which after all would perhaps have been as beautiful and interesting, if we only had a mind to see it so.

The short, comparatively swift-flowing Hoffman Glacier, whose fountains extend along the south slopes of the Hoffman Range, offered a striking contrast to the one just described. The erosive energy of the latter was diffused over a wide field of sunken, boulder-like domes and ridges. The Hoffman Glacier, on the contrary, moved right ahead on a comparatively even surface, making a descent of nearly five thousand feet in five miles, steadily contracting and deepening its current, and finally united with the Tenaya Glacier as one of its most influential tributaries in the development and sculpture of the great Half Dome, North Dome and the rocks adjacent to them about the head of the Valley.

The story of its death is not unlike that of its companion already described, though the declivity of its channel, and its uniform exposure to sun-heat prevented any considerable portion of its current from becoming torpid, lingering only well up on the mountain slopes to finish their sculpture and encircle them with a zone of moraine soil for forests and gardens. Nowhere in all this wonderful region will you find more beautiful trees and shrubs and flowers covering the traces of ice.

The rugged Tenaya Glacier wildly crevassed here and there above the ridges it had to cross, instead of drawing its sources direct from the summit of the range, formed, as we have seen, one of the outlets of the great Tuolumne Glacier, issuing from this noble fountain like a river from a lake, two miles wide, about fourteen miles long, and from 1500 to 2000 feet deep.

In leaving the Tuolumne region it crossed over the divide, as mentioned above, between the Tuolumne and Tenaya basins, making an ascent of five hundred feet. Hence, after contracting its wide current and receiving a strong affluent from the fountains about Cathedral Peak, it poured its massive flood over the northeastern rim of its basin in splendid cascades. Then, crushing heavily against the Clouds Rest Ridge, it bore down upon the Yosemite domes with concentrated energy.

Toward the end of the ice period, while its Hoffman companion continued to grind rock-meal for coming plants, the main trunk became torpid, and vanished, exposing wide areas of rolling rock-waves and glistening pavements, on whose channel-less surface water ran wild and free. And because the trunk vanished almost simultaneously throughout its whole extent, no terminal moraines are found in its canyon channel; nor, since its walls are, in most places, too steeply inclined to admit of the deposition of moraine matter, do we find much of the two main laterals. The lowest of its residual glaciers lingered beneath the shadow of the Yosemite Half Dome; others along the base of

Coliseum Peak above Lake Tenaya and along the precipitous wall extending from the lake to the Big Tuolumne Meadows. The latter, on account of the uniformity and continuity of their protecting shadows, formed moraines of considerable length and regularity that are liable to be mistaken for portions of the left lateral of the Tuolumne tributary glacier.

Spend all the time you can spare or steal on the tracks of this grand old glacier, charmed and enchanted by its magnificent canyon, lakes and cascades and resplendent glacier pavements.

The Nevada Glacier was longer and more symmetrical than the last, and the only one of the Merced system whose sources extended directly back to the main summits on the axis of the range. Its numerous fountains were ranged side by side in three series, at an elevation of from 10,000 to 12,000 feet above the sea. The first, on the right side of the basin, extended from the Matterhorn to Cathedral Peak; that on the left through the Merced Group, and these two parallel series were united by a third that extended around the head of the basin in a direction at right angles to the others.

The three ranges of high peaks and ridges that supplied the snow for these fountains, together with the Clouds Rest Ridge, nearly inclose a rectangular basin, that was filled with a massive sea of ice, leaving an outlet toward the west through which flowed the main trunk glacier, three-fourths of a mile to a mile and a half wide, fifteen miles long, and from 1000 to 1500 feet deep, and entered Yosemite between the Half Dome and Mount Starr King.

Could we have visited Yosemite Valley at this period of its history, we should have found its ice cascades vastly more glorious than their tiny water representatives of the present day. One of the grandest of these was formed by that portion of the Nevada Glacier that poured over the shoulder of the Half Dome.

This glacier, as a whole, resembled an oak, with a gnarled swelling base and wide-spreading branches. Picturesque rocks of every conceivable form adorned its banks, among which glided the numerous tributaries, mottled with black and red and gray boulders, from the fountain peaks, while ever and anon, as the deliberate centuries passed away, dome after dome raised its burnished crown above the ice-flood to enrich the slowly opening landscapes.

The principal moraines occur in short irregular sections along the sides of the canyons, their fragmentary condition being due to interruptions caused by portions of the sides of the canyon walls being too steep for moraine matter to lie on, and to down-sweeping torrents and avalanches. The left lateral of the trunk may be traced about five miles from the mouth of the first main tributary to the Illilouette Canyon. The corresponding section of the right lateral, extending from Cathedral tributary to the Half Dome, is more complete because of the more favorable character of the north side of the canyon. A short side-glacier came in against it from the slopes of Clouds Rest; but being fully exposed to the sun, it was melted long before the main trunk, allowing the latter to deposit this portion of its moraine undisturbed. Some conception of the size and appearance of this fine moraine may be gained by following the Clouds Rest trail from Yosemite, which crosses it obliquely and conducts past several sections made by streams. Slate boulders may be seen that must have come from the Lyell Group, twelve miles distant. But the bulk of the moraine is composed of porphyritic granite derived from Feldspar and Cathedral Valleys.

On the sides of the moraines we find a series of terraces, indicating fluctuations in the level of the glacier, caused by variations of snowfall, temperature, etc., showing that the climate of the glacial period was diversified by cycles of milder or stormier seasons similar to those of post-glacial time.

After the depth of the main trunk diminished to about five hundred feet, the greater portion became torpid, as is shown by the moraines, and lay dying in its crooked channel like a wounded snake, maintaining for a time a feeble squirming motion in places of exceptional depth, or where the bottom of the canyon was more steeply inclined. The numerous fountain-wombs, however, continued fruitful long after the trunk had vanished, giving rise to an imposing array of short residual glaciers, extending around the rim of the general basin a distance of nearly twenty-four miles. Most of these have but recently succumbed to the new climate, dying in turn as determined by elevation, size, and exposure, leaving only a few feeble survivors beneath the coolest shadows, which are now slowly completing the sculpture of one of the noblest of the Yosemite basins.

The comparatively shallow glacier that at this time filled the Illilouette Basin, though once far from shallow, more resembled a lake than a river of ice, being nearly half as wide as it was long. Its greatest length was about ten miles, and its depth perhaps nowhere much exceeded 1000 feet. Its chief fountains, ranged along the west side of the Merced Group, at an elevation of about 10,000 feet, gave birth to fine tributaries that flowed in a westerly direction, and united in the center of the basin. The broad trunk at first flowed northwestward, then curved to the northward, deflected by the lofty wall forming its western bank, and finally united with the grand Yosemite trunk, opposite Glacier Point.

All the phenomena relating to glacial action in this basin are remarkably simple and orderly, on account of the sheltered positions occupied by its ice-fountains, with reference to the disturbing effects of larger glaciers from the axis of the main range earlier in the period. From the eastern base of the Starr King cone you may obtain a fine view of the principal moraines sweeping grandly out into the middle of the basin from the shoulders of the peaks, between which the ice-fountains lay. The right lateral of the tributary, which took its rise between Red and Merced Mountains, measures two hundred and fifty feet in height at its upper extremity, and displays three well-defined terraces, similar to those of the South Lyell Glacier. The comparative smoothness of the uppermost terrace shows that it is considerably more ancient than the others, many of the boulders of which it is composed having crumbled. A few miles to the westward, this moraine has an average slope of twenty-seven degrees, and an elevation above the bottom of the channel of six hundred and sixty feet. Near the middle of the main basin, just where the regularly formed medial and lateral moraines flatten out and disappear, there is a remarkably smooth field of gravel, planted with arctostaphylos, that looks at the distance of a mile like a delightful meadow. Stream sections show the gravel deposit to be composed of the same material as the moraines, but finer, and more water-worn from the action of converging torrents issuing from the tributary glaciers after the trunk was melted. The southern boundary of the basin is a strikingly perfect wall, gray on the top, and white down the sides and at the base with snow, in which many a crystal brook takes rise. The northern boundary is made up of smooth undulating masses of gray granite, that lift here and there into beautiful domes of which the Starr King cluster is the

finest, while on the east tower the majestic fountain-
peaks with wide canyons and névé amphitheaters between them, whose variegated rocks show out gloriously against the sky.

The ice-plows of this charming basin, ranged side
by side in orderly gangs, furrowed the rocks with admirable uniformity, producing irrigating channels for a
brood of wild streams, and abundance of rich soil
adapted to every requirement of garden and grove.
No other section of the Yosemite uplands is in so perfect a state of glacial cultivation. Its domes, and peaks,
and swelling rock-waves, however majestic in themselves, are yet submissively subordinate to the garden
center. The other basins we have been describing are
combinations of sculptured rocks, embellished with
gardens and groves; the Illilouette is one grand garden
and forest, embellished with rocks, each of the five
beautiful in its own way, and all as harmoniously related as are the five petals of a flower. After uniting in
the Yosemite Valley, and expending the down-thrusting energy derived from their combined weight and
the declivity of their channels, the grand trunk flowed
on through and out of the Valley. In effecting its exit
a considerable ascent was made, traces of which may
still be seen on the abraded rocks at the lower end of
the Valley, while the direction pursued after leaving
the Valley is surely indicated by the immense lateral
moraines extending from the ends of the walls at an
elevation of from 1500 to 1800 feet. The right lateral
moraine was disturbed by a large tributary glacier that
occupied the basin of Cascade Creek, causing considerable complication in its structure. The left is simple
in form for several miles of its length, or to the point
where a tributary came in from the southeast. But
both are greatly obscured by the forests and under-
brush growing upon them, and by the denuding action of rains and melting snows, etc. It is, therefore,

the less to be wondered at that these moraines, made up of material derived from the distant fountain-mountains, and from the Valley itself, were not sooner recognized.

The ancient glacier systems of the Tuolumne, San Joaquin, Kern, and Kings River basins were developed on a still grander scale and are so replete with interest that the most sketchy outline descriptions of each, with the works they have accomplished, would fill many a volume. Therefore I can do but little more than invite everybody who is free to go and see for himself.

The action of flowing ice, whether in the form of river-like glaciers or broad mantles, especially the part it played in sculpturing the earth, is as yet but little understood. Water rivers work openly where people dwell, and so does the rain, and the sea, thundering on all the shores of the world; and the universal ocean of air, though invisible, speaks aloud in a thousand voices, and explains its modes of working and its power. But glaciers, back in their white solitudes, work apart from men, exerting their tremendous energies in silence and darkness. Outspread, spirit-like, they brood above the predestined landscapes, work on unwearied through immeasurable ages, until, in the fullness of time, the mountains and valleys are brought forth, channels furrowed for rivers, basins made for lakes and meadows, and arms of the sea, soils spread for forests and fields; then they shrink and vanish like summer clouds.[4]

[4] Matthes paid tribute to Muir's contributions to knowledge of the influence of glaciers in sculpturing the Yosemite and other Sierra canyons. But it is now known that the Sierra Nevada and other Western ranges were not overridden by the great continental glaciers of the Ice Age. They were separate centers of glaciation, during four successive periods separated by long intervals of normal climate. Muir underestimated the effects of earth movements and stream erosion in cutting the canyons, and of massive granite in shaping domes.

XII

HOW BEST TO SPEND ONE'S YOSEMITE TIME

ONE-DAY EXCURSIONS[1]
No. 1.

If I were so time-poor as to have only one day to spend in Yosemite I should start at daybreak, say at three o'clock in midsummer, with a pocketful of any sort of dry breakfast stuff, for Glacier Point, Sentinel Dome, the head of Illilouette Fall, Nevada Fall, the top of Liberty Cap, Vernal Fall and the wild boulder-choked River Canyon. The trail[2] leaves the Valley at the base of the Sentinel Rock, and as you slowly saunter from point to point along its many accommodating zigzags nearly all the Valley rocks and falls are seen in striking, ever-changing combinations. At an elevation of about five hundred feet a particularly fine, wide-sweeping view down the Valley is obtained, past the sheer face of the Sentinel and between the Cathedral Rocks and El Capitan. At a height of about 1500 feet the great Half Dome comes full in sight, overshadowing every other feature of the Valley to the eastward. From Glacier Point you look down 3000 feet

---

[1] Muir was a prodigy of speed, agility and ascetic devotion to mountain pursuits. Ordinary hikers, even those who are muscular and experienced, should take his timetables with a grain of skepticism. See the notes following each Excursion, and consult maps, *Starr's Guide*, and the rangers. Keep to trails, or follow a good leader.

[2] Glacier Point-Fourmile Trail.

over the edge of its sheer face to the meadows and groves and innumerable yellow pine spires, with the meandering river sparkling and spangling through the midst of them. Across the Valley a great telling view is presented of the Royal Arches, North Dome, Indian Canyon, Three Brothers and El Capitan, with the dome-paved basin of Yosemite Creek and Mount Hoffman in the background. To the eastward, the Half Dome close beside you looking higher and more wonderful than ever; southeastward the Starr King, girdled with silver firs, and the spacious garden-like basin of the Illilouette and its deeply sculptured fountain-peaks, called "The Merced Group"; and beyond all, marshaled along the eastern horizon, the icy summits on the axis of the range and broad swaths of forests growing on ancient moraines, while the Nevada, Vernal and Yosemite Falls are not only full in sight but are distinctly heard as if one were standing beside them in their spray.

The views from the summit of Sentinel Dome are still more extensive and telling. Eastward the crowds of peaks at the head of the Merced, Tuolumne and San Joaquin Rivers are presented in bewildering array; westward, the vast forests, yellow foothills and the broad San Joaquin plains and the Coast Ranges, hazy and dim in the distance.

From Glacier Point go down the trail into the lower end of the Illilouette Basin, cross Illilouette Creek and follow it to the Fall where from an out-jutting rock at its head you will get a fine view of its rejoicing waters and wild canyon and the Half Dome. Thence returning to the trail, follow it to the head of the Nevada Fall. Linger here an hour or two, for not only have you glorious views of the wonderful Fall, but of its wild, leaping, exulting rapids and, greater than all, the stupendous scenery into the heart of which the white passionate river goes wildly thundering, surpassing everything of its kind in the world. After an unmeasured hour or so of this glory, all your body aglow, nerve currents flashing through you never before felt, go to the top of the Liberty Cap, only a glad saunter now that your legs as well as head and heart are awake and rejoicing with everything. The Liberty Cap, a companion of the Half Dome, is sheer and inaccessible on three of its sides but on the east a gentle, ice-burnished, juniper-dotted slope extends to the summit where other wonderful views are displayed where all are wonderful: the south side and shoulders of Half Dome and Clouds Rest, the beautiful Little Yosemite Valley and its many domes, the Starr King cluster of domes, Sentinel Dome, Glacier Point, and, perhaps the most tremendously impressive of all, the views of the hopper-shaped canyon of the river from the head of the Nevada Fall to the head of the Valley.

Returning to the trail you descend between the Nevada Fall and the Liberty Cap with fine side views of both the Fall and the rock, pass on through clouds of spray and along the rapids to the head of the Vernal Fall, about a mile below the Nevada. Linger here if night is still distant, for views of this favorite Fall and the stupendous rock scenery about it. Then descend a stairway by its side, follow a dim trail through its spray, and a plain one along the border of the boulder-dashed rapids and so back to the wide, tranquil Valley.[3]

ONE-DAY EXCURSIONS
No. 2.

Another grand one-day excursion is to the Upper Yosemite Fall, the top of the highest of the Three

[3] Round-trip distance from Park Headquarters (in Yosemite Village), by trail, about 24 miles.

Brothers, called Eagle Peak on the Geological Survey maps; the brow of El Capitan; the head of the Ribbon Fall; across the beautiful Ribbon Creek Basin; and back to the Valley by the Big Oak Flat wagon-road.

The trail leaves the Valley on the east side of the largest of the earthquake taluses immediately opposite the Sentinel Rock and as it passes within a few rods of the foot of the great Fall, magnificent views are obtained as you approach it and pass through its spray, though when the snow is melting fast you will be well drenched. From the foot of the Fall the trail zigzags up a narrow canyon between the Fall and a plain mural cliff that is burnished here and there by glacial action.

You should stop a while on a flat iron-fenced rock a little below the head of the Fall beside the enthusiastic throng of starry comet-like waters to learn something of their strength, their marvelous variety of forms, and above all, their glorious music, gathered and composed from the snowstorms, hail-, rain- and wind-storms that have fallen on their glacier-sculptured, domey, ridgy basin. Refreshed and exhilarated, you follow your trail-way through silver fir and pine woods to Eagle Peak, where the most comprehensive of all the views to be had on the north-wall heights are displayed. After an hour or two of gazing, dreaming, studying the tremendous topography, etc., trace the rim of the Valley to the grand El Capitan ridge and go down to its brow, where you will gain everlasting impressions of Nature's steadfastness and power combined with ineffable fineness of beauty.

Dragging yourself away, go to the head of the Ribbon Fall, thence across the beautiful Ribbon Creek Basin to the Big Oak Flat stage-road, and down its fine grades to the Valley, enjoying glorious Yosemite scenery all the way to the foot of El Capitan and your camp.[4]

TWO-DAY EXCURSIONS
No. 1.

For a two-day trip I would go straight to Mount Hoffman, spend the night on the summit, next morning go down by May Lake to Tenaya Lake and return to the Valley by Clouds Rest and the Nevada and Vernal Falls. As on the foregoing excursion, you leave the Valley by the Yosemite Falls trail and follow it to the Tioga wagon-road, a short distance east of Porcupine Flat. From that point push straight up to the summit. Mount Hoffman is a mass of gray granite that rises almost in the center of the Yosemite Park, about eight or ten miles in a straight line from the Valley. Its southern slopes are low and easily climbed, and adorned here and there with castle-like crumbling piles and long jagged crests that look like artificial masonry; but on the north side it is abruptly precipitous and banked with lasting snow. Most of the broad summit is comparatively level and thick sown with crystals, quartz, mica, hornblende, feldspar, granite, zircon, tourmaline, etc., weathered out and strewn closely and loosely as if they had been sown broadcast. Their radiance is fairly dazzling in sunlight, almost hiding the multitude of small flowers that grow among them. At first sight only these radiant crystals are likely to be noticed, but looking closely you discover a multitude of very small gilias, phloxes, mimulus, etc., many of them with more petals than leaves. On the borders of little streams larger plants flourish

[4] Round-trip distance from Park Headquarters, by trail, returning via the Old Big Oak Flat Road and roads and paths in the Valley, about 24 miles.

—lupines, daisies, asters, goldenrods, hairbell,[5] mountain columbine, potentilla, astragalus and a few gentians; with charming heathworts—bryanthus,[6] cassiope, kalmia, vaccinium in boulder-fringing rings or
bank covers. You saunter among the crystals and
flowers as if you were walking among stars. From the
summit nearly all the Yosemite Park is displayed like
a map: forests, lakes, meadows, and snowy peaks.
Northward lies Yosemite's wide basin with its domes
and small lakes, shining like larger crystals; eastward
the rocky, meadowy Tuolumne region, bounded by its
snowy peaks in glorious array; southward Yosemite
and westward the vast forest. On no other Yosemite
Park mountain are you more likely to linger. You will
find it a magnificent sky camp. Clumps of dwarf pine
and mountain hemlock will furnish resin roots and
branches for fuel and light, and the rills, sparkling
water. Thousands of the little plant people will gaze
at your campfire with the crystals and stars, companions and guardians as you lie at rest in the heart of the
vast serene night.

The most telling of all the wide Hoffman views is
the basin of the Tuolumne with its meadows, forests
and hundreds of smooth rock-waves that appear to be
coming rolling on towards you like high heaving waves
ready to break, and beyond these the great mountains.
But best of all are the dawn and the sunrise. No mountain top could be better placed for this most glorious of
mountain views—to watch and see the deepening colors of the dawn and the sunbeams streaming through
the snowy High Sierra passes, awakening the lakes
and crystals, the chilled plant people and winged peo-

[5] A puzzling reference even if spelled harebell, although
Campanula prenanthoides is found at lower elevations.
[6] *Phyllodoce.*

ple, and making everything shine and sing in pure glory.

With your heart aglow, spangling Lake Tenaya and Lake May will beckon you away for walks on their ice-burnished shores. Leave Tenaya at the west end, cross to the south side of the outlet, and gradually work your way up in an almost straight south direction to the summit of the divide between Tenaya Creek and the main upper Merced River or Nevada Creek and follow the divide to Clouds Rest. After a glorious view from the crest of this lofty granite wave you will find a trail on its western end that will lead you down past Nevada and Vernal Falls to the Valley in good time, provided you left your Hoffman sky camp early.[7]

TWO-DAY EXCURSIONS
No. 2.

Another grand two-day excursion is the same as the first of the one-day trips, as far as the head of Illilouette Fall. From there trace the beautiful stream up through the heart of its magnificent forests and gardens to the canyons between the Red and Merced Peaks, and pass the night where I camped forty-one years ago. Early next morning visit the small glacier on the north side of Merced Peak, the first of the sixty-five that I discovered in the Sierra.

Glacial phenomena in the Illilouette Basin are on the grandest scale, and in the course of my explorations I found that the canyon and moraines between the Merced and Red Mountains were the most interesting of them all. The path of the vanished glacier shone in many places as if washed with silver, and pushing up the canyon on this bright road I passed lake

[7] Round-trip distance from Park Headquarters, by trails where possible, about 38 miles.

after lake in solid basins of granite and many a
meadow along the canyon stream that links them together. The main lateral moraines that bound the view
below the canyon are from a hundred to nearly two
hundred feet high and wonderfully regular, like artificial embankments, covered with a magnificent
growth of silver fir and pine. But this garden and
forest luxuriance is speedily left behind, and patches
of bryanthus, cassiope and arctic willows begin to
appear. The small lakes which a few miles down the
Valley are so richly bordered with flowery meadows
have at an elevation of 10,000 feet only small brown
mats of carex, leaving bare rocks around more than
half their shores. Yet, strange to say, amid all this
arctic repression the mountain pine on ledges and buttresses of Red Mountain seems to find the climate best
suited to it. Some specimens that I measured were
over a hundred feet high and twenty-four feet in circumference, showing hardly a trace of severe storms,
looking as fresh and vigorous as the giants of the lower
zones. Evening came on just as I got fairly into the
main canyon. It is about a mile wide and a little less
than two miles long. The crumbling spurs of Red
Mountain bound it on the north, the somber cliffs of
Merced Mountain on the south and a deeply-serrated,
splintered ridge curving around from mountain to
mountain shuts it in on the east. My camp was on the
brink of one of the lakes in a thicket of mountain hemlock, partly sheltered from the wind. Early next morning I set out to trace the ancient glacier to its head.
Passing around the north shore of my camp lake I
followed the main stream from one lakelet to another.
The dwarf pines and hemlocks disappeared and the
stream was bordered with icicles. The main lateral
moraines that extend from the mouth of the canyon
are continued in straggling masses along the walls.

Tracing the streams back to the highest of its little lakes, I noticed a deposit of fine gray mud, something like the mud worn from a grindstone. This suggested its glacial origin, for the stream that was carrying it issued from a raw-looking moraine that seemed to be in process of formation. It is from sixty to over a hundred feet high in front, with a slope of about thirty-eight degrees. Climbing to the top of it, I discovered a very small but well-characterized glacier swooping down from the shadowy cliffs of the mountain to its terminal moraine. The ice appeared on all the lower portion of the glacier; farther up it was covered with snow. The uppermost crevasse or "bergschrund" was from twelve to fourteen feet wide. The melting snow and ice formed a network of rills that ran gracefully down the surface of the glacier, merrily singing in their shining channels. After this discovery I made excursions over all the High Sierra and discovered that what at first sight looked like snow-fields were in great part glaciers which were completing the sculpture of the summit-peaks.

Rising early,—which will be easy, as your bed will be rather cold and you will not be able to sleep much anyhow,—after visiting the glacier, climb the Red Mountain and enjoy the magnificent views from the summit. I counted forty lakes from one standpoint on this mountain, and the views to the westward over the Illilouette Basin, the most superbly forested of all the basins whose waters drain into Yosemite, and those of the Yosemite rocks, especially the Half Dome and the upper part of the north wall, are very fine. But, of course, far the most imposing view is the vast array of snowy peaks along the axis of the range. Then from the top of this peak, light and free and exhilarated with mountain air and mountain beauty, you should run lightly down the northern slope of the mountain, descend the canyon between Red and Gray Mountains, thence northward along the bases of Gray Mountain and Mount Clark and go down into the head of Little Yosemite, and thence down past the Nevada and Vernal Falls to the Valley, a truly glorious two-day trip![8]

A THREE-DAY EXCURSION

The best three-day excursion, as far as I can see, is the same as the first of the two-day trips until you reach Lake Tenaya. There instead of returning to the Valley, follow the Tioga Road around the northwest side of the lake, over to the Tuolumne Meadows and up to the west base of Mount Dana. Leave the road there and make straight for the highest point on the timberline between Mounts Dana and Gibbs and camp there.

On the morning of the third day go to the top of Mount Dana in time for the glory of the dawn and the sunrise over the gray Mono Desert and the sublime forest of High Sierra peaks. When you leave the mountain go far enough down the north side for a view of the Dana Glacier, then make your way back to the Tioga Road, follow it along the Tuolumne Meadows to the crossing of Budd Creek where you will find the Sunrise Trail branching off up the mountain-side through the forest in a southwesterly direction past the west side of Cathedral Peak, which will lead you down to the Valley by the Vernal and Nevada Falls. If you are a good walker you can leave the trail where it begins to descend a steep slope in the silver fir woods, and bear off to the right and make straight for the top of Clouds Rest. The walking is good and almost level and from the west end of Clouds Rest

[8] Round-trip distance from Park Headquarters, much of the return across country without trails, about 50 miles.

take the Clouds Rest trail which will lead direct to
the Valley by the Nevada and Vernal Falls. To anyone not desperately time-poor this trip should have
four days instead of three; camping the second night
at the Soda Springs; thence to Mount Dana and return
to the Soda Springs, camping the third night there;
thence by the Sunrise Trail to Cathedral Peak, visiting
the beautiful Cathedral Lake which lies about a mile
to the west of Cathedral Peak, eating your luncheon,
and thence to Clouds Rest and the Valley as above.
This is one of the most interesting of all the comparatively short trips that can be made in the whole Yosemite region. Not only do you see all the grandest of the
Yosemite rocks and waterfalls and the High Sierra with
their glaciers, glacier lakes and glacier meadows, etc.,
but sections of the magnificent silver fir, two-leaved
pine, and dwarf pine zones; with the principal alpine
flowers and shrubs, especially sods of dwarf vaccinium[9] covered with flowers and fruit though less than
an inch high, broad mats of dwarf willow[10] scarce an
inch high with catkins that rise straight from the
ground, and glorious beds of blue gentians,[11]—grandeur enough and beauty enough for a lifetime.[12]

THE UPPER TUOLUMNE EXCURSION

We come now to the grandest of all the Yosemite
excursions, one that requires at least two or three
weeks. The best time to make it is from about the

[9] *Vaccinium caespitosum.*

[10] *Salix anglorum,* var. *antiplasta* (known until recently as
S. *petrophila,* var. *caespitosa*).

[11] *Gentiana holopetala.*

[12] Round-trip distance from Park Headquarters, by trails
where possible but by Tioga Road from Lake Tenaya to
Tuolumne Meadows, more than 60 miles! As Muir hints, this
is a three-day trip only for the desperately time-poor. Others
would be well advised to invest a full week in this route, with
variations.

middle of July. The visitor entering the Yosemite in July has the advantage of seeing the falls not, perhaps, in their very flood prime but next thing to it; while the glacier-meadows will be in their glory and the snow on the mountains will be firm enough to make climbing safe. Long ago I made these Sierra trips, carrying only a sackful of bread with a little tea and sugar and was thus independent and free, but now that trails or carriage roads lead out of the Valley in almost every direction it is easy to take a pack animal, so that the luxury of a blanket and a supply of food can easily be had.

The best way to leave the Valley will be by the Yosemite Fall trail, camping the first night on the Tioga Road opposite the east end of the Hoffman Range. Next morning climb Mount Hoffman; thence push on past Tenaya Lake into the Tuolumne Meadows and establish a central camp near the Soda Springs, from which glorious excursions can be made at your leisure. For here in this upper Tuolumne Valley is the widest, smoothest, most serenely spacious, and in every way the most delightful summer pleasure-park in all the High Sierra. And since it is connected with Yosemite by two good trails, and a fairly good carriage road that passes between Yosemite and Mount Hoffman, it is also the most accessible.[13] It is in the heart of the High Sierra east of Yosemite, 8500 to 9000 feet above the level of the sea. The gray, picturesque Cathedral Range bounds it on the south; a similar range or spur, the highest peak of which is Mount Conness, on the north; the noble Mounts Dana, Gibbs, Mammoth, Lyell, McClure and others on the axis of the range on the east; a heaving, billowy crowd

[13] From Park Headquarters to Tuolumne Meadows by auto, via Big Oak Flat Road to Crane Flat and thence via Tioga Road, about 55 miles.

of glacier-polished rocks and Mount Hoffman on the west. Down through the open sunny meadow-levels of the Valley flows the Tuolumne River, fresh and cool from its many glacial fountains, the highest of which are the glaciers that lie on the north sides of Mount Lyell and Mount McClure.

Along the river a series of beautiful glacier-meadows extend with but little interruption, from the lower end of the Valley to its head, a distance of about twelve miles, forming charming sauntering-grounds from which the glorious mountains may be enjoyed as they look down in divine serenity over the dark forests that clothe their bases. Narrow strips of pine woods cross the meadow-carpet from side to side, and it is somewhat roughened here and there by moraine boulders and dead trees brought down from the heights by snow avalanches; but for miles and miles it is so smooth and level that a hundred horsemen may ride abreast over it.

The main lower portion of the meadows is about four miles long and from a quarter to half a mile wide; but the width of the Valley is, on an average, about eight miles. Tracing the river, we find that it forks a mile above the Soda Springs, the main fork turning southward to Mount Lyell, the other eastward to Mount Dana and Mount Gibbs. Along both forks strips of meadow extend almost to their heads. The most beautiful portions of the meadows are spread over lake basins, which have been filled up by deposits from the river. A few of these river-lakes still exist, but they are now shallow and are rapidly approaching extinction. The sod in most places is exceedingly fine and silky and free from weeds and bushes; while charming flowers abound, especially gentians, dwarf daisies, potentillas, and the pink bells of dwarf vaccinium. On the banks of the river and its tributaries cassiope and

bryanthus[14] may be found, where the sod curls over
stream banks and around boulders. The principal grass
of these meadows is a delicate calamagrostis[15] with
very slender filiform leaves, and when it is in flower
the ground seems to be covered with a faint purple
mist, the stems of the panicles being so fine that they
are almost invisible, and offer no appreciable resistance in walking through them. Along the edges of
the meadows beneath the pines and throughout the
greater part of the Valley tall ribbon-leaved grasses
grow in abundance, chiefly bromus, triticum and
agrostis.[16]

In October the nights are frosty, and then the meadows at sunrise, when every leaf is laden with crystals,
are a fine sight. The days are still warm and calm,
and bees and butterflies continue to waver and hum
about the late-blooming flowers until the coming of
the snow, usually in November. Storm then follows
storm in quick succession, burying the meadows to a
depth of from ten to twenty feet, while magnificent
avalanches descend through the forests from the laden
heights, depositing huge piles of snow mixed with
uprooted trees and boulders. In the open sunshine the
snow usually lasts until the end of June but the new
season's vegetation is not generally in bloom until late
in July. Perhaps the best all-round excursion-time
after winters of average snowfall is from the middle of
July to the middle or end of August. The snow is
then melted from the woods and southern slopes of the
mountains and the meadows and gardens are in their
glory, while the weather is mostly all-reviving, exhilarating sunshine. The few clouds that rise now and

14 *Phyllodoce.*
15 *Calamagrostis Breweri.*
16 Triticum: *Agropyron.* Agrostis: *Calamagrostis canadensis.*

then and the showers they yield are only enough to keep everything fresh and fragrant.

The groves about the Soda Springs are favorite camping-grounds[17] on account of the cold, pleasant-tasting water charged with carbonic acid, and because of the views of the mountains across the meadow—the Glacier Monument,[18] Cathedral Peak, Unicorn Peak and a series of ornamental nameless companions, rising in striking forms and nearness above a dense forest growing on the left lateral moraine of the ancient Tuolumne Glacier, which, broad, deep, and far-reaching, exerted vast influence on the scenery of this portion of the Sierra. But there are fine camping-grounds all along the meadows, and one may move from grove to grove every day all summer, enjoying new homes and new beauty to satisfy every roving desire for change.[19]

There are five main capital excursions to be made from here—to the summits of Mounts Dana, Lyell and Conness, and through the Bloody Canyon Pass to Mono Lake and the volcanoes, and down the Tuolumne Canyon, at least as far as the foot of the wonderful series of river cataracts. All of these excursions are sure to be made memorable with joyful health-giving experiences; but perhaps none of them will be remembered with keener delight than the days spent in sauntering on the broad velvet lawns by the river, sharing the sky with the mountains and trees, gaining something of their strength and peace.

The excursion to the top of Mount Dana is a very easy one; for though the mountain is 13,000 feet high, the ascent from the west side is so gentle and smooth

[17] Property of the Sierra Club since 1912.
[18] Fairview Dome.
[19] Tuolumne Meadows has been developed as one of the Park's principal camping centers. During the summer months sites are in heavy demand.

that one may ride a mule to the very summit. Across
many a busy stream, from meadow to meadow, lies
your flowery way; mountains all about you, few of
them hidden by irregular foregrounds. Gradually ascending, other mountains come in sight, peak rising
above peak with their snow and ice in endless variety
of grouping and sculpture. Now your attention is
turned to the moraines, sweeping in beautiful curves
from the hollows and canyons, now to the granite
waves and pavements rising here and there above the
heathy sod, polished a thousand years ago and still
shining. Towards the base of the mountain you note
the dwarfing of the trees, until at a height of about
11,000 feet you find patches of the tough, whitebarked
pine, pressed so flat by the ten or twenty feet of snow
piled upon them every winter for centuries that you
may walk over them as if walking on a shaggy rug.
And, if curious about such things, you may discover
specimens of this hardy tree-mountaineer not more
than four feet high and about as many inches in diameter at the ground, that are from two hundred to four
hundred years old, still holding bravely to life, making
the most of their slender summers, shaking their tas-
sled needles in the breeze right cheerily, drinking the
thin sunshine and maturing their fine purple cones
as if they meant to live forever. The general view from
the summit is one of the most extensive and sublime
to be found in all the range. To the eastward you
gaze far out over the desert plains and mountains of
the "Great Basin," range beyond range extending with
soft outlines, blue and purple in the distance. More
than six thousand feet below you lies Lake Mono, ten
miles in diameter from north to south, and fourteen
from west to east, lying bare in the treeless desert like
a disk of burnished metal, though at times it is swept
by mountain storm-winds and streaked with foam. To

the southward there is a well-defined range of pale-gray extinct volcanoes, and though the highest of them rises nearly two thousand feet above the lake, you can look down from here into their circular, cup-like craters, from which a comparatively short time ago ashes and cinders were showered over the surrounding sage plains and glacier-laden mountains.

To the westward the landscape is made up of exceedingly strong, gray, glaciated domes and ridge waves, most of them comparatively low, but the largest high enough to be called mountains; separated by canyons and darkened with lines and fields of forest, Cathedral Peak and Mount Hoffman in the distance; small lakes and innumerable meadows in the foreground. Northward and southward the great snowy mountains, marshaled along the axis of the range, are seen in all their glory, crowded together in some places like trees in groves, making landscapes of wild, extravagant, bewildering magnificence, yet calm and silent as the sky.

Some eight glaciers are in sight. One of these is the Dana Glacier on the north side of the mountain, lying at the foot of a precipice about a thousand feet high, with a lovely pale-green lake a little below it. This is one of the many, small, shrunken remnants of the vast glacial system of the Sierra that once filled the hollows and valleys of the mountains and covered all the lower ridges below the immediate summit-fountains, flowing to right and left away from the axis of the range, lavishly fed by the snows of the glacial period.

In the excursion to Mount Lyell the immediate base of the mountain is easily reached on meadow walks along the river. Turning to the southward above the forks of the river, you enter the narrow Lyell branch of the valley, narrow enough and deep enough to be called a canyon. It is about eight miles long and from 2000 to 3000 feet deep. The flat meadow bottom is from about three hundred to two hundred yards wide, with gently curved margins about fifty yards wide from which rise the simple massive walls of gray granite at an angle of about thirty-three degrees, mostly timbered with a light growth of pine and streaked in many places with avalanche channels. Towards the upper end of the canyon the Sierra crown comes in sight, forming a finely balanced picture framed by the massive canyon walls. In the foreground, when the grass is in flower, you have the purple meadow willow-thickets on the river banks; in the middle distance huge swelling bosses of granite that form the base of the general mass of the mountain, with fringing lines of dark woods marking the lower curves, smoothly snow-clad except in the autumn.

If you wish to spend two days on the Lyell trip you will find a good camp-ground on the east side of the river, about a mile above a fine cascade that comes down over the canyon wall in telling style and makes good camp music. From here to the top of the mountains is usually an easy day's work. At one place near the summit careful climbing is necessary, but it is not so dangerous or difficult as to deter anyone of ordinary skill, while the views are glorious. To the northward are Mammoth Peak, Mounts Gibbs, Dana, Warren, Conness and others, unnumbered and unnamed; to the southeast the indescribably wild and jagged range of Mount Ritter and the Minarets; southwestward stretches the dividing ridge between the north fork of the San Joaquin and the Merced, uniting with the Obelisk or Merced Group of peaks that form the main fountains of the Illilouette branch of the Merced; and to the northwestward extends the Cathedral spur. These spurs like distinct ranges meet at your feet; therefore you look them mostly in the direction of their extension, and their peaks seem to be massed and crowded against one another, while immense amphitheaters, canyons and subordinate ridges with their wealth of lakes, glaciers, and snow-fields, maze and cluster between them. In making the ascent in June or October the glacier is easily crossed, for then its snow mantle is smooth or mostly melted off. But in midsummer the climbing is exceedingly tedious because the snow is then weathered into curious and beautiful blades, sharp and slender, and set on edge in a leaning position. They lean towards the head of the glacier and extend across from side to side in regular order in a direction at right angles to the direction of greatest declivity, the distance between the crests being about two or three feet, and the depth of the troughs between them about three feet. A more interesting problem than a walk over a glacier thus sculptured and adorned is seldom presented to the mountaineer.

The Lyell Glacier is about a mile wide and less than a mile long, but presents, nevertheless, all the essential characters of large, river-like glaciers—moraines, earth-bands, blue veins, crevasses, etc., while the streams that issue from it are, of course, turbid with rock-mud, showing its grinding action on its bed. And it is all the more interesting since it is the highest and most enduring remnant of the great Tuolumne Glacier, whose traces are still distinct fifty miles away, and whose influence on the landscape was so profound. The McClure Glacier, once a tributary of the Lyell, is smaller. Thirty-eight years ago I set a series of stakes in it to determine its rate of motion. Towards the end of summer in the middle of the glacier it was only a little over an inch in twenty-four hours.

The trip to Mono from the Soda Springs can be

made in a day,[20] but many days may profitably be
spent near the shores of the lake, out on its islands and
about the volcanoes.

In making the trip down the Big Tuolumne Canyon, animals may be led as far as a small, grassy, forested lake-basin that lies below the crossing of the
Virginia Creek trail. And from this point anyone accustomed to walking on earthquake boulders, car-
peted with canyon chaparral, can easily go down as
far as the big cascades and return to camp in one day.
Many, however, are not able to do this, and it is
better to go leisurely, prepared to camp anywhere,
and enjoy the marvelous grandeur of the place.

The canyon begins near the lower end of the meadows and extends to the Hetch Hetchy Valley, a distance of about eighteen miles, though it will seem
much longer to anyone who scrambles through it.
It is from twelve hundred to about five thousand feet
deep, and is comparatively narrow, but there are several roomy, park-like openings in it, and throughout its
whole extent Yosemite features are displayed on a
grand scale—domes, El Capitan rocks, gables, Sentinels,
Royal Arches, Glacier Points, Cathedral Spires, etc.
There is even a Half Dome among its wealth of rock
forms, though far less sublime than the Yosemite Half
Dome. Its falls and cascades are innumerable. The
sheer falls, except when the snow is melting in early
spring, are quite small in volume as compared with
those of Yosemite and Hetch Hetchy; though in any
other country many of them would be regarded as
wonders. But it is the cascades or sloping falls on the
main river that are the crowning glory of the canyon,
and these in volume, extent and variety surpass those
of any other canyon in the Sierra. The most showy and
interesting of them are mostly in the upper part of

[20] Less than an hour by auto.

the canyon, above the point of entrance of Cathedral
Creek and Hoffman Creek. For miles the river is
one wild, exulting, on-rushing mass of snowy purple
bloom, spreading over glacial waves of granite without
any definite channel, gliding in magnificent silver
plumes, dashing and foaming through huge boulder-
dams, leaping high into the air in wheel-like whirls,
displaying glorious enthusiasm, tossing from side to
side, doubling, glinting, singing in exuberance of
mountain energy.

Everyone who is anything of a mountaineer should
go on through the entire length of the canyon, coming
out by Hetch Hetchy. There is not a dull step all the
way. With wide variations, it is a Yosemite Valley from
end to end.[21]

Besides these main, far-reaching, much-seeing excursions from the main central camp, there are num-
berless, lovely little saunters and scrambles and a dozen
or so not so very little. Among the best of these are to
Lembert and Fairview Domes; to the topmost spires
of Cathedral Peak, and to those of the North Church,[22]
around the base of which you pass on your way to
Mount Conness; to one of the very loveliest of the
glacier meadows imbedded in the pine woods about
three miles north of the Soda Springs, where forty-two
years ago I spent six weeks. It trends east and west,
and you can find it easily by going past the base of
Lembert Dome to Dog Lake and thence up northward
through the woods about a mile or so; to the shining
rock-waves full of ice-burnished, feldspar crystals at
the foot of the meadows; to Lake Tenaya; and, last
but not least, a rather long and very hearty scramble

[21] The backwater of Hetch Hetchy reservoir attracts few
travelers. There is a trail down the Tuolumne, skirting Muir
Gorge, which climbs up to Harden Lake from Pate Valley.
As far as Pate Valley, Muir's comments are still valid.
[22] Ragged Peak.

down by the end of the meadow along the Tioga Road toward Lake Tenaya to the crossing of Cathedral Creek, where you turn off and trace the creek down to its confluence with the Tuolumne. This is a genuine scramble much of the way but one of the most wonderfully telling in its glacial rock-forms and inscriptions.

If you stop and fish at every tempting lake and stream you come to, a whole month, or even two months, will not be too long for this grand High Sierra excursion. My own Sierra trip was ten years long.

OTHER TRIPS FROM THE VALLEY

Short carriage trips are usually made in the early morning to Mirror Lake to see its wonderful reflections of the Half Dome and Mount Watkins;[23] and in the afternoon many ride down the Valley to see the Bridal Veil rainbows or up the river canyon to see those of the Vernal Fall; where, standing in the spray, not minding getting drenched, you may see what are called round rainbows, when the two ends of the ordinary bow are lengthened and meet at your feet, forming a complete circle which is broken and united again and again as determined by the varying wafts of spray. A few ambitious scramblers climb to the top of the Sentinel Rock, others walk or ride down the Valley and up to the once-famous Inspiration Point for a last grand view; while a good many appreciative tourists, who have only a day or two, do no climbing or riding but spend their time sauntering on the meadows by the river, watching the falls, and the play of light and shade among the rocks from morning to night, perhaps gaining more than those who make haste up the trails in large noisy parties. Those who have unlimited time find something worth while all the year

[23] Mirror Lake is gradually filling with silt and vegetation. It is much smaller than it was in Muir's time.

round on every accessible part of the vast, deeply sculptured walls. At least so I have found it after making the Valley my home for years.

Here are a few specimens selected from my own short trips which walkers may find useful.

One, up the river canyon, across the bridge between the Vernal and Nevada Falls, through chaparral beds and boulders to the shoulder of Half Dome, along the top of the shoulder to the dome itself, down by a crumbling slot gully and close along the base of the tremendous split front (the most awfully impressive, sheer, precipice view I ever found in all my canyon wanderings), thence up the east shoulder and along the ridge to Clouds Rest—a glorious sunset—then a grand starry run back home to my cabin; down through the junipers, down through the firs, now in black shadows, now in white light, past roaring Nevada and Vernal, glowering ghost-like beneath their huge frowning cliffs; down the dark, gloomy canyon, through the pines of the Valley, dreamily murmuring in their calm, breezy sleep—a fine wild little excursion for good legs and good eyes—so much sun-, moon- and star-shine in it, and sublime, up-and-down rhythmical, glacial topography.

Another, to the head of Yosemite Fall by Indian Canyon[24] thence up the Yosemite Creek, tracing it all the way to its highest sources back of Mount Hoffman, then a wide sweep around the head of its dome-paved basin, passing its many little lakes and bogs, gardens and groves, trilling, warbling rills, and back by the Fall Canyon. This was one of my Sabbath walk, run-and-slide excursions long ago before any trail had been made on the north side of the Valley.

[24] The old trail in Indian Canyon is almost obliterated by Nature. There is an unmaintained trail from the head of the canyon to Yosemite Point and a trace from there to Yosemite Fall.

Another fine trip was up, bright and early, by Avalanche Canyon to Glacier Point,[25] along the rugged south wall, tracing all its far outs and ins to the head of the Bridal Veil Fall, thence back home, bright and late, by a brushy, bouldery slope between Cathedral Rocks and Cathedral Spires and along the level Valley floor. This was one of my long, bright-day and bright-night walks thirty or forty years ago when, like river and ocean currents, time flowed undivided, uncounted —a fine free, sauntery, scrambly, botanical, beauty-filled ramble. The walk up the Valley was made glorious by the marvelous brightness of the morning star. So great was her light, she made every tree cast a well-defined shadow on the smooth sandy ground.

Everybody who visits Yosemite wants to see the famous Big Trees. Before the railroad was constructed, all three of the stage-roads that entered the Valley passed through a grove of these trees by the way; namely, the Tuolumne, Merced and Mariposa groves. The Tuolumne Grove was passed on the Big Oak Flat Road, the Merced Grove by the Coulterville road and the Mariposa Grove by the Raymond and Wawona road. Now, to see any one of these groves, a special trip has to be made. Most visitors go to the Mariposa Grove, the largest of the three. On this Sequoia trip you see not only the giant Big Trees but magnificent forests of silver fir, sugar pine, yellow pine, libocedrus and Douglas spruce. The trip need not require more than two days, spending a night in a good hotel at Wawona, a beautiful place on the south fork of the Merced River, and returning to the Valley or to El Portal, the terminus of the railroad. This extra

[25] Perhaps via the route of the Ledge Trail, a steep ascent from Camp Curry. The trail is no longer maintained, and climbers intending to use it must inform the rangers as with any rock climb.

trip by stage costs fifteen dollars. All the High Sierra excursions that I have sketched cost from a dollar a week to anything you like. None of mine when I was exploring the Sierra cost over a dollar a week, most of them less.[26]

[26] The stagecoach routes gave way in 1907 to the Yosemite Valley Railroad, which ran from Merced to El Portal until World War II. Meanwhile the automobile had become the common means of travel. Prices, of course, have undergone vast changes in a half-century. The cost of transportation in Muir's time is to be found in Appendix C at the end of this book.

Today, knapsack hikers still enjoy the back country frugally, while other travelers burn high-octane fuel and eat and sleep more expensively at the resorts.

XIII

EARLY HISTORY OF THE VALLEY

In the wild gold years of 1849 and '50, the Indian tribes along the western Sierra foothills became alarmed at the sudden invasion of their acorn orchard and game fields by miners, and soon began to make war upon them, in their usual murdering, plundering style. This continued until the United States Indian Commissioners succeeded in gathering them into reservations, some peacefully, others by burning their villages and stores of food. The Yosemite or Grizzly Bear tribe, fancying themselves secure in their deep mountain stronghold, were the most troublesome and defiant of all, and it was while the Mariposa battalion, under command of Major Savage, was trying to capture this war-like tribe and conduct them to the Fresno reservation that their deep mountain home, the Yosemite Valley, was discovered. From a camp on the south fork of the Merced, Major Savage sent Indian runners to the bands who were supposed to be hiding in the mountains, instructing them to tell the Indians that if they would come in and make treaty with the Commissioners they would be furnished with food and clothing and be protected, but if they did not come in he would make war upon them and kill them all. None of the Yosemite Indians responded to this general message, but when a special messenger was sent to the chief he appeared the next day. He came entirely alone and stood in dignified silence before one of the guards until invited to enter the camp. He was recognized by one of the friendly Indians as Tenaya, the old chief of the Grizzlies, and, after he had been supplied with food, Major Savage, with the aid of Indian interpreters, informed him of the wishes of the Commissioners. But the old chief was very suspicious of Savage and feared that he was taking this method of getting the tribe into his power for the purpose of revenging his personal wrong. Savage told him if he would go to the Commissioners and make peace with them as the other tribes had done there would be no more war. Tenaya inquired what was the object of taking all the Indians to the San Joaquin plain. "My people," said he, "do not want anything from the Great Father you tell me about. The Great Spirit is our father and he has always supplied us with all we need. We do not want anything from white men. Our women are able to do our work. Go, then. Let us remain in the mountains where we were born, where the ashes of our fathers have been given to the wind. I have said enough."

To this the Major answered abruptly in Indian style: "If you and your people have all you desire, why do you steal our horses and mules? Why do you rob the miners' camps? Why do your murder the white men and plunder and burn their houses?"

Tenaya was silent for some time. He evidently understood what the Major had said, for he replied, "My young men have sometimes taken horses and mules from the whites. This was wrong. It is not wrong to take the property of enemies who have wronged my people. My young men believed that the gold diggers were our enemies. We now know they are not and we shall be glad to live in peace with them. We will stay here and be friends. My people do not want to go to the plains. Some of the tribes who have gone there are very bad. We cannot live with them. Here we can defend ourselves."

To this Major Savage firmly said, "Your people must go to the Commissioners. If they do not your young men will again steal horses and kill and plunder the whites. It was your people who robbed my stores, burned my houses and murdered my men. If they do not make a treaty, your whole tribe will be destroyed. Not one of them will be left alive."

To this the old chief replied, "It is useless to talk to you about who destroyed your property and killed your people. I am old and you can kill me if you will, but it is useless to lie to you who know more than all the Indians. Therefore I will not lie to you but if you will let me return to my people I will bring them in." He was allowed to go. The next day he came back and said his people were on the way to our camp to go with the men sent by the Great Father, who was so good and rich.

Another day passed but no Indians from the deep Valley appeared. The old chief said that the snow was so deep and his village was so far down that it took a long time to climb out of it. After waiting still another day the expedition started for the Valley. When Tenaya was questioned as to the route and distance he said that the snow was so deep that the horses could not go through it. Old Tenaya was taken along as guide. When the party had gone about half-way to the Valley they met the Yosemites on their way to the camp on the south fork. There were only seventy-two of them and when the old chief was asked what had become of the rest of his band, he replied, "This is all of my people that are willing to go with me to the plains. All the rest have gone with their wives and children over the mountains to the Mono and Tuolumne tribes." Savage told Tenaya that he was not telling the truth, for Indians could not cross the mountains in the deep snow, and that he knew they must still be at his village or hiding somewhere near it. The tribe had been estimated to number over two hundred. Major Savage then said to him, "You may return to camp with your people and I will take one of your young men with me to your village to see your people who will not come. They will come if I find them." "You will not find any of my people there," said Tenaya; "I do not know where they are. My tribe is small. Many of the people of my tribe have come from other tribes and if they go to the plains and are seen they will be killed by the friends of those with whom they have quarreled. I was told that I was growing old and it was well that I should go, but that young and strong men can find plenty in the mountains: therefore, why should they go to the hot plains to be penned up like horses and cattle? My heart has been sore since that talk but I am now willing to go, for it is best for my people."

Pushing ahead, taking turns in breaking a way through the snow, they arrived in sight of the great Valley early in the afternoon and, guided by one of Tenaya's Indians, descended by the same route as that followed by the Mariposa trail, and the weary party went into camp on the river bank opposite El Capitan. After supper, seated around a big fire, the wonderful Valley became the topic of conversation and Dr. Bunnell suggested giving it a name. Many were proposed, but after a vote had been taken the name Yosemite, proposed by Dr. Bunnell, was adopted almost unanimously to perpetuate the name of the tribe who so long had made their home there. The Indian name of the Valley, however, is Ahwahnee. The Indians had names for all the different rocks and streams of the Valley, but very few of them are now in use by the whites, Pohono, the Bridal Veil, being the principal one. The expedition remained only one day and two nights in the Valley, hurrying out on the approach of a storm and reached the south-fork headquarters on the evening of the third day after starting out. Thus, in three days the round trip had been made to the Valley, most of it had been explored in a general way and some of its principal features had been named. But the Indians had fled up the Tenaya Canyon trail and none of them were seen, except an old woman unable to follow the fugitives.

A second expedition was made in the same year under command of Major Boling. When the Valley was entered no Indians were seen, but the many wigwams with smoldering fires showed that they had been hurriedly abandoned that very day. Later, five young Indians who had been left to watch the movements of the expedition were captured at the foot of the Three Brothers after a lively chase. Three of the five were sons of the old chief and the rock was named for them. All of these captives made good their escape within a few days, except the youngest son of Tenaya, who was shot by his guard while trying to escape. That same day the old chief was captured on the cliff on the east side of Indian Canyon by some of Boling's scouts. As Tenaya walked toward the camp his eye fell upon the dead body of his favorite son. Captain Boling through an interpreter, expressed his regret at the occurrence, but not a word did Tenaya utter in reply. Later, he made an attempt to escape but was caught as he was about to swim across the river. Tenaya expected to be shot for this attempt and when brought into the presence of Captain Boling he said in great emotion, "Kill me, Sir Captain, yes, kill me as you killed my son, as you would kill my people if they were to come to you. You would kill all my tribe if you had the power. Yes, Sir America, you can now tell your warriors to kill the old chief. You have made my life dark with sorrow. You killed the child of my heart. Why not kill the father? But wait a little and when I am dead I will call my people to come and they shall hear me in their sleep and come to avenge the death of their chief and his son. Yes, Sir America, my spirit will make trouble for you and your people, as you have made trouble to me and my people. With the wizards I will follow the white people and make them fear me. You may kill me, Sir Captain, but you shall not live in peace. I will follow in your footsteps. I will not leave my home, but be with the spirits among the rocks, the waterfalls, in the rivers and in the winds; wherever you go I will be with you. You will not see me but you will fear the spirit of the old chief and grow cold. The Great Spirit has spoken. I am done."

This expedition finally captured the remnants of the tribes at the head of Lake Tenaya and took them to the Fresno reservation, together with their chief, Tenaya. But after a short stay they were allowed to return to the Valley under restrictions. Tenaya promised faithfully to conform to everything required, joyfully left the hot and dry reservation, and with his family returned to his Yosemite home.

The following year a party of miners was attacked by the Indians in the Valley and two of them were killed. This led to another Yosemite expedition. A detachment of regular soldiers from Fort Miller under Lieutenant Moore, U. S. A., was at once dispatched to capture or punish the murderers. Lieutenant Moore entered the Valley in the night and surprised and captured a party of five Indians, but an alarm was given and Tenaya and his people fled from their huts and escaped to the Monos on the east side of the range. On examination of the five prisoners in the morning it was discovered that each of them had some article of clothing that belonged to the murdered men. The bodies of the two miners were found and buried on the edge of the Bridal Veil meadow. When the captives were accused of the murder of the two white men they admitted that they had killed them to prevent white men from coming to their Valley, declaring that it was their home and that white men had no right to come there without their consent. Lieutenant Moore told them through his interpreter that they had sold their lands to the Government, that it belonged to the white men now, and that they had agreed to live on the reservation provided for them. To this they replied that Tenaya had never consented to the sale of their Valley and had never received pay for it. The other chief, they said, had no right to sell their territory. The lieutenant being fully satisfied that he had captured the real murderers, promptly pronounced judgment and had them placed in line and shot. Lieutenant Moore pursued the fugitives to Mono but was not successful in finding any of them. After being hospitably entertained and protected by the Mono and Paiute tribes, they stole a number of stolen horses from their entertainers and made their way by a long, obscure route by the head of the north fork of the San Joaquin, reached their Yosemite home once more, but early one morning, after a feast of horse-flesh, a band of Monos surprised them in their huts, killing Tenaya and nearly all his tribe. Only a small remnant escaped down the river canyon. The Tenaya Canyon and Lake were named for the famous old chief.

Very few visits were made to the Valley before the summer of 1855, when Mr. J. M. Hutchings, having heard of its wonderful scenery, collected a party and made the first regular tourist's visit to the Yosemite and in his California magazine described it in articles

illustrated by a good artist, who was taken into the
Valley by him for that purpose. This first party was
followed by another from Mariposa the same year,
consisting of sixteen or eighteen persons. The next
year the regular pleasure travel began and a trail on
the Mariposa side of the Valley was opened by Mann
Brothers. This trail was afterwards purchased by the
citizens of the county and made free to the public. The
first house built in the Yosemite Valley was erected in
the autumn of 1856 and was kept as a hotel the next
year by G. A. Hite and later by J. H. Neal and S. M.
Cunningham. It was situated directly opposite the Yosemite Fall. A little over half a mile farther up the
Valley a canvas house was put up in 1858 by G. A.
Hite. Next year a frame house was built and kept as a
hotel by Mr. Peck, afterward by Mr. Longhurst and
since 1864 by Mr. Hutchings. All these hotels have
vanished except the frame house built in 1859, which
has been changed beyond recognition. A large hotel
built on the brink of the river in front of the old one is
now the only hotel in the Valley. A large hotel built
by the State and located farther up the Valley was
burned. To provide for the overflow of visitors there
are three camps with board floors, wood frame, and
covered with canvas, well furnished, some of them
with electric light. A large first-class hotel is very much
needed.[1]

Travel of late years has been rapidly increasing,
especially after the establishment, by Act of Congress
in 1890, of the Yosemite National Park and the recession in 1905 of the original reservation to the Federal
Government by the State. The greatest increase, of

[1] Hotel and cabin facilities are provided in the Valley and
outside it by the Yosemite Park and Curry Co. Some are first-
class. The modern problem is not a shortage of rooms (though
it is wise to make advance reservations), but the pressure of
crowds on the available open space.

course, was caused by the construction of the Yosemite Valley Railroad from Merced to the border of the Park, eight miles below the Valley.

It is eighty miles long, and the entire distance, except the first twenty-four miles from the town of Merced, is built through the precipitous Merced River Canyon. The roadbed was virtually blasted out of the solid rock for the entire distance in the canyon. Work was begun in September, 1905, and the first train entered El Portal, the terminus, April 15, 1907. Many miles of the road cost as much as $100,000 per mile. Its business has increased from 4000 tourists in the first year it was operated to 15,000 in 1910.[2]

[2] Over the years the railroad lost passenger traffic to automobiles, and other economic changes in addition to heavy flood damage in 1937 brought an end to its usefulness. The tracks were removed in 1945. El Portal is now the site of Park and concessioner employee residences and is a base of service operations for Park Headquarters.

XIV

LAMON

The good old pioneer, Lamon, was the first of all the early Yosemite settlers who cordially and unreservedly adopted the Valley as his home.

He was born in the Shenandoah Valley, Virginia, May 10, 1817, emigrated to Illinois with his father, John Lamon, at the age of nineteen; afterwards went to Texas and settled on the Brazos, where he raised melons and hunted alligators for a living. "Right interestin' business," he said; "especially the alligator part of it." From the Brazos he went to the Comanche Indian country between Gonzales and Austin, twenty miles from his nearest neighbor. During the first summer, the only bread he had was the breast meat of wild turkeys. When the formidable Comanche Indians were on the war-path he left his cabin after dark and slept in the woods. From Texas he crossed the plains to California and worked in the Calaveras and Mariposa gold-fields.

He first heard Yosemite spoken of as a very beautiful mountain valley and after making two excursions in the summers of 1857 and 1858 to see the wonderful place, he made up his mind to quit roving and make a permanent home in it. In April, 1859, he moved into it, located a garden opposite the Half Dome, set out a lot of apple, pear and peach trees, planted potatoes, etc., that he had packed in on a "contrary old mule," and worked for his board in building a hotel which was afterwards purchased by Mr. Hutchings. His

neighbors thought he was very foolish in attempting
to raise crops in so high and cold a valley, and warned
him that he could raise nothing and sell nothing, and
would surely starve.

For the first year or two lack of provisions compelled him to move out on the approach of winter, but
in 1862 after he had succeeded in raising some fruit
and vegetables he began to winter in the Valley.

The first winter he had no companions, not even a
dog or cat, and one evening was greatly surprised to
see two men coming up the Valley. They were very
glad to see him, for they had come from Mariposa in
search of him, a report having been spread that he had
been killed by Indians. He assured his visitors that he
felt safer in his Yosemite home, lying snug and
squirrel-like in his 10 x 12 cabin than in Mariposa.
When the avalanches began to slip, he wondered
where all the wild roaring and booming came from,
the flying snow preventing them from being seen. But,
upon the whole, he wondered most at the brightness,
gentleness, and sunniness of the weather, and hope-
fully employed the calm days in clearing ground for
an orchard and vegetable garden.

In the second winter he built a winter cabin under
the Royal Arches, where he enjoyed more sunshine.
But no matter how he praised the weather he could
not induce anyone to winter with him until 1864.

He liked to describe the great flood of 1867, the
year before I reached California, when all the walls
were striped with thundering waterfalls.

He was a fine, erect, whole-souled man, between six
and seven feet high, with a broad, open face, bland
and guileless as his pet oxen. No stranger to hunger
and weariness, he knew well how to appreciate suf-
fering of a like kind in others, and many there be, myself among the number, who can testify to his simple,

unostentatious kindness that found expression in a
thousand small deeds.

After gaining sufficient means to enjoy a long afternoon of life in comparative affluence and ease, he died
in the autumn of 1876. He sleeps in a beautiful spot
near Galen Clark and a monument hewn from a block
of Yosemite granite marks his grave.

XV
GALEN CLARK

Galen Clark was the best mountaineer I ever met, and one of the kindest and most amiable of all my mountain friends. I first met him at his Wawona ranch forty-three years ago on my first visit to Yosemite. I had entered the Valley with one companion by way of Coulterville, and returned by what was then known as the Mariposa trail. Both trails were buried in deep snow where the elevation was from 5000 to 7000 feet above sea-level in the sugar pine and silver fir regions. We had no great difficulty, however, in finding our way by the trends of the main features of the topography. Botanizing by the way, we made slow, plodding progress, and were again about out of provisions when we reached Clark's hospitable cabin at Wawona. He kindly furnished us with flour and a little sugar and tea, and my companion, who complained of the benumbing poverty of a strictly vegetarian diet, gladly accepted Mr. Clark's offer of a piece of a bear that had just been killed. After a short talk about bears and the forests and the way to the Big Trees, we pushed on up through the Wawona firs and sugar pines, and camped in the now-famous Mariposa Grove.

Later, after making my home in the Yosemite Valley, I became well acquainted with Mr. Clark, while he was Guardian. He was elected again and again to this important office by different Boards of Commissioners on account of his efficiency and his real love of the Valley.

Although nearly all my mountaineering has been done without companions, I had the pleasure of having Galen Clark with me on three excursions. About thirty-five years ago I invited him to accompany me on a trip through the Big Tuolumne Canyon from Hetch Hetchy Valley. The canyon up to that time had not been explored, and knowing that the difference in the elevation of the river at the head of the canyon and in Hetch Hetchy was about 5000 feet, we expected to find some magnificent cataracts or falls; nor were we disappointed. When we were leaving Yosemite an ambitious young man begged leave to join us. I strongly advised him not to attempt such a long, hard trip, for it would undoubtedly prove very trying to an inexperienced climber. He assured us, however, that he was equal to anything, would gladly meet every difficulty as it came, and cause us no hindrance or trouble of any sort. So at last, after repeating our advice that he give up the trip, we consented to his joining us. We entered the canyon by way of Hetch Hetchy Valley, each carrying his own provisions, and making his own tea, porridge, bed, etc.

In the morning of the second day out from Hetch Hetchy we came to what is now known as "Muir Gorge," and Mr. Clark without hesitation prepared to force a way through it, wading and jumping from one submerged boulder to another through the torrent, bracing and steadying himself with a long pole. Though the river was then rather low, the savage, roaring, surging song it was singing was rather nerve-trying, especially to our inexperienced companion. With careful assistance, however, I managed to get him through, but this hard trial, naturally enough, proved too much and he informed us, pale and trembling, that he could go no farther. I gathered some wood at the upper throat of the gorge, made a fire for him and advised him to feel at home and make himself comfortable, hoped he would enjoy the grand scenery and the songs of the water-ouzels which haunted the gorge, and assured him that we would return some time in the night, though it might be late, as we wished to go on through the entire canyon if possible. We pushed our way through the dense chaparral and over the earthquake taluses with such speed that we reached the foot of the upper cataract while we had still an hour or so of daylight for the return trip. It was long after dark when we reached our adventurous, but nerve-shaken companion who, of course, was anxious and lonely, not being accustomed to solitude, however kindly and flowery and full of sweet bird-song and stream-song. Being tired we simply lay down in restful comfort on the river bank beside a good fire, instead of trying to go down the gorge in the dark or climb over its high shoulder to our blankets and provisions, which we had left in the morning in a tree at the foot of the gorge. I remember Mr. Clark remarking that if he had his choice that night between provisions and blankets he would choose his blankets.

The next morning in about an hour we had crossed over the ridge through which the gorge is cut, reached our provisions, made tea, and had a good breakfast. As soon as we had returned to Yosemite I obtained fresh provisions, pushed off alone up to the head of Yosemite Creek basin, entered the canyon by a side canyon, and completed the exploration up to the Tuolumne Meadows.

It was on this first trip from Hetch Hetchy to the upper cataracts that I had convincing proofs of Mr. Clark's daring and skill as a mountaineer, particularly in fording torrents, and in forcing his way through thick chaparral. I found it somewhat difficult to keep up with him in dense, tangled brush, though in jumping on boulder taluses and slippery cobble-beds I had no difficulty in leaving him behind.

After I had discovered the glaciers on Mount Lyell and Mount McClure, Mr. Clark kindly made a second excursion with me to assist in establishing a line of stakes across the McClure glacier to measure its rate of flow. On this trip we also climbed Mount Lyell together, when the snow which covered the glacier was melted into upleaning, icy blades which were extremely difficult to cross, not being strong enough to support our weight, nor wide enough apart to enable us to stride across each blade as it was met. Here again I, being lighter, had no difficulty in keeping ahead of him. While resting after wearisome staggering and falling he stared at the marvelous ranks of leaning blades, and said, "I think I have traveled all sorts of trails and canyons, through all kinds of brush and snow, but this gets me."

Mr. Clark at my urgent request joined my small party on a trip to the Kings River yosemite by way of the high mountains, most of the way without a trail. He joined us at the Mariposa Big Tree Grove and intended to go all the way, but finding that, on account of the difficulties encountered, the time required was much greater than he expected, he turned back near the head of the north fork of the Kings River.

In cooking his mess of oatmeal porridge and making tea, his pot was always the first to boil, and I used to wonder why, with all his skill in scrambling through brush in the easiest way, and preparing his meals, he was so utterly careless about his beds. He would lie down anywhere on any ground, rough or smooth, without taking pains even to remove cobbles or sharp-angled rocks protruding through the grass or gravel, saying that his own bones were as hard as any stones and could do him no harm.

His kindness to all Yosemite visitors and mountaineers was marvelously constant and uniform. He was not a good business man, and in building an extensive hotel and barns at Wawona, before the travel to Yosemite had been greatly developed, he borrowed money, mortgaged his property and lost it all.

Though not the first to see the Mariposa Big Tree Grove, he was the first to explore it, after he had heard from a prospector, who had passed through the grove and who gave him the indefinite information, that there were some wonderful Big Trees up there on the top of the Wawona hill and that he believed they must be of the same kind that had become so famous and well-known in the Calaveras Grove farther north. On this information, Galen Clark told me, he went up and thoroughly explored the grove, counting the trees and measuring the largest, and becoming familiar with it. He stated also that he had explored the forest to the southward and had discovered the much larger Fresno Grove of about two square miles, six or seven miles distant from the Mariposa Grove. Unfortunately most of the Fresno Grove had been cut and flumed down to the railroad near Madera.

Mr. Clark was truly and literally a gentle-man. I never heard him utter a hasty, angry, fault-finding word. His voice was uniformly pitched at a rather low tone, perfectly even, although glances of his eyes and slight intonations of his voice often indicated that something funny or mildly sarcastic was coming, but upon the whole he was serious and industrious, and, however deep and fun-provoking a story might be, he never indulged in boisterous laughter.

He was very fond of scenery and once told me after I became acquainted with him that he liked "nothing in the world better than climbing to the top of a high ridge or mountain and looking off." He preferred the mountain ridges and domes in the Yosemite regions on account of the wealth and beauty of the forests. Oftentimes he would take his rifle, a few pounds of bacon, a few pounds of flour, and a single blanket and go off hunting, for no other reason than to explore and get acquainted with the most beautiful points of view within a journey of a week or two from his Wawona home. On these trips he was always alone and could indulge in tranquil enjoyment of Nature to his heart's content. He said that on those trips, when he was a sufficient distance from home in a neighborhood where he wished to linger, he always shot a deer, sometimes a grouse, and occasionally a bear. After diminishing the weight of a deer or bear by eating part of it, he carried as much as possible of the best of the meat to Wawona, and from his hospitable well-supplied cabin no weary wanderer ever went away hungry or unrested.

The value of the mountain air in prolonging life is well exemplified in Mr. Clark's case. While working in the mines he contracted a severe cold that settled on his lungs and finally caused severe inflammation and bleeding, and none of his friends thought he would ever recover. The physicians told him he had but a short time to live. It was then that he repaired to the beautiful sugar pine woods at Wawona and took up a claim, including the fine meadows there, and building his cabin, began his life of wandering and exploring in the glorious mountains about him, usually going bareheaded. In a remarkably short time his lungs were healed.

He was one of the most sincere tree-lovers I ever knew. About twenty years before his death he made choice of a plot in the Yosemite cemetery on the north side of the Valley, not far from the Yosemite Fall, and selecting a dozen or so of seedling sequoias in the Mariposa Grove he brought them to the Valley and planted them around the spot he had chosen for his last rest. The ground there is gravelly and dry; by careful watering he finally nursed most of the seedlings into good, thrifty trees, and doubtless they will long shade the grave of their blessed lover and friend.

XVI

HETCH HETCHY VALLEY

Yosemite is so wonderful that we are apt to regard it as an exceptional creation, the only valley of its kind in the world; but Nature is not so poor as to have only one of anything. Several other yosemites have been discovered in the Sierra that occupy the same relative positions on the range and were formed by the same forces in the same kind of granite. One of these, the Hetch Hetchy Valley, is in the Yosemite National Park about twenty miles from Yosemite and is easily accessible to all sorts of travelers by a road and trail that leaves the Big Oak Flat Road at Bronson Meadows a few miles below Crane Flat, and to mountaineers by way of Yosemite Creek basin and the head of the middle fork of the Tuolumne.[1]

It is said to have been discovered by Joseph Screech, a hunter, in 1850, a year before the discovery of the great Yosemite. After my first visit to it in the autumn of 1871, I have always called it the "Tuolumne Yosemite," for it is a wonderfully exact counterpart of the Merced Yosemite, not only in its sublime rocks and waterfalls but in the gardens, groves and meadows of its flowery park-like floor. The floor of Yosemite is about 4000 feet above the sea; the Hetch Hetchy floor about 3700 feet. And as the Merced River flows through Yosemite, so does the Tuolumne through

[1] Hetch Hetchy Valley is flooded by a reservoir. (See note, p. 202.) The dam is reached by auto from the Big Oak Flat highway, via Mather.

Hetch Hetchy. The walls of both are of gray granite, rise abruptly from the floor, are sculptured in the same style and in both every rock is a glacier monument.

Standing boldly out from the south wall is a strikingly picturesque rock called by the Indians, Kolana, the outermost of a group 2300 feet high, corresponding with the Cathedral Rocks of Yosemite both in relative position and form. On the opposite side of the Valley, facing Kolana, there is a counterpart of the El Capitan that rises sheer and plain to a height of 1800 feet, and over its massive brow flows a stream which makes the most graceful fall I have ever seen. From the edge of the cliff to the top of an earthquake talus it is perfectly free in the air for a thousand feet before it is broken into cascades among talus boulders. It is in all its glory in June, when the snow is melting fast, but fades and vanishes toward the end of summer. The only fall I know with which it may fairly be compared is the Yosemite Bridal Veil; but it excels even that favorite fall both in height and airy-fairy beauty and behavior. Lowlanders are apt to suppose that mountain streams in their wild career over cliffs lose control of themselves and tumble in a noisy chaos of mist and spray. On the contrary, on no part of their travels are they more harmonious and self-controlled. Imagine yourself in Hetch Hetchy on a sunny day in June, standing waist-deep in grass and flowers (as I have often stood), while the great pines sway dreamily with scarcely perceptible motion. Looking northward across the Valley you see a plain, gray granite cliff rising abruptly out of the gardens and groves to a height of 1800 feet, and in front of it Tueeulala's silvery scarf burning with irised sun-fire. In the first white outburst at the head there is abundance of visible energy, but it is speedily hushed and concealed in divine repose, and its tranquil progress to the base of the cliff is like

that of a downy feather in a still room. Now observe
the fineness and marvelous distinctness of the various
sun-illumined fabrics into which the water is woven;
they sift and float from form to form down the face of
that grand gray rock in so leisurely and unconfused a
manner that you can examine their texture, and patterns and tones of color as you would a piece of embroidery held in the hand. Toward the top of the fall
you see groups of booming, comet-like masses, their
solid, white heads separate, their tails like combed
silk interlacing among delicate gray and purple shadows, ever forming and dissolving, worn out by friction in their rush through the air. Most of these vanish
a few hundred feet below the summit, changing to
varied forms of cloud-like drapery. Near the bottom
the width of the fall has increased from about twenty-
five feet to a hundred feet. Here it is composed of yet
finer tissues, and is still without a trace of disorder—
air, water and sunlight woven into stuff that spirits
might wear.

So fine a fall might well seem sufficient to glorify
any valley; but here, as in Yosemite, Nature seems in
nowise moderate, for a short distance to the eastward
of Tueeulala booms and thunders the great Hetch
Hetchy Fall, Wapama, so near that you have both of
them in full view from the same standpoint. It is the
counterpart of the Yosemite Fall, but has a much
greater volume of water, is about 1700 feet in height,
and appears to be nearly vertical, though considerably
inclined, and is dashed into huge outbounding bosses
of foam on projecting shelves and knobs. No two falls
could be more unlike—Tueeulala out in the open sunshine descending like thistledown; Wapama in a
jagged, shadowy gorge roaring and thundering,
pounding its way like an earthquake avalanche.

Besides this glorious pair there is a broad, massive

fall on the main river a short distance above the head of the Valley. Its position is something like that of the Vernal in Yosemite, and its roar as it plunges into a surging trout-pool may be heard a long way, though it is only about twenty feet high. On Rancheria Creek, a large stream, corresponding in position with the Yosemite Tenaya Creek, there is a chain of cascades joined here and there with swift flashing plumes like the one between the Vernal and Nevada Falls, making magnificent shows as they go their glacier-sculptured way, sliding, leaping, hurrahing, covered with crisp clashing spray made glorious with sifting sunshine. And besides all these a few small streams come over the walls at wide intervals, leaping from ledge to ledge with bird-like song and watering many a hidden cliff-garden and fernery, but they are too unshowy to be noticed in so grand a place.

The correspondence between the Hetch Hetchy walls in their trends, sculpture, physical structure, and general arrangement of the main rock-masses and those of the Yosemite Valley has excited the wondering admiration of every observer. We have seen that the El Capitan and Cathedral Rocks occupy the same relative positions in both valleys; so also do their Yosemite points and North Domes. Again, that part of the Yosemite north wall immediately to the east of the Yosemite Fall has two horizontal benches, about 500 and 1500 feet above the floor, timbered with golden-cup oak. Two benches similarly situated and timbered occur on the same relative portion of the Hetch Hetchy north wall, to the east of Wapama Fall, and on no other. The Yosemite is bounded at the head by the great Half Dome. Hetch Hetchy is bounded in the same way, though its head rock is incomparably less wonderful and sublime in form.

The floor of the Valley is about three and a half miles long, and from a fourth to half a mile wide. The lower portion is mostly a level meadow about a mile long, with the trees restricted to the sides and the river banks, and partially separated from the main, upper, forested portion by a low bar of glacier-polished granite across which the river breaks in rapids.

The principal trees are the yellow and sugar pines, digger pine, incense cedar, Douglas spruce, silver fir, the California and golden-cup oaks, balsam cottonwood, Nuttall's flowering dogwood, alder, maple, laurel, tumion, etc.[2] The most abundant and influential are the great yellow or silver pines like those of Yosemite, the tallest over two hundred feet in height, and the oaks assembled in magnificent groves with massive rugged trunks four to six feet in diameter, and broad, shady, wide-spreading heads. The shrubs forming conspicuous flowery clumps and tangles are manzanita, azalea, spiræa, brier-rose, several species of ceanothus, calycanthus, philadelphus, wild cherry, etc.; with abundance of showy and fragrant herbaceous plants growing about them or out in the open in beds by themselves—lilies, Mariposa tulips, brodiaeas, orchids, iris, spraguea, draperia, collomia, collinsia, castilleja, nemophila, larkspur, columbine, goldenrods, sunflowers, mints of many species, honeysuckle, etc. Many fine ferns dwell here also, especially the beautiful and interesting rock-ferns—pellaea, and cheilanthes of several species—fringing and rosetting dry rock-piles and ledges; woodwardia and asplenium[3] on damp spots with fronds six or seven feet high; the delicate maidenhair in mossy nooks by the falls, and the sturdy,

[2] Douglas spruce: Douglas fir. California oak: California black oak. Balsam cottonwood: Black cottonwood. Tumion: California nutmeg, *Torreya californica.*
[3] Athyrium.

broad-shouldered pteris[4] covering nearly all the dry ground beneath the oaks and pines.

It appears, therefore, that Hetch Hetchy Valley, far from being a plain, common, rock-bound meadow, as many who have not seen it seem to suppose, is a grand landscape garden, one of Nature's rarest and most precious mountain temples. As in Yosemite, the sublime rocks of its walls seem to glow with life, whether leaning back in repose or standing erect in thoughtful attitudes, giving welcome to storms and calms alike, their brows in the sky, their feet set in the groves and gay flowery meadows, while birds, bees, and butterflies help the river and waterfalls to stir all the air into music—things frail and fleeting and types of permanence meeting here and blending, just as they do in Yosemite, to draw her lovers into close and confiding communion with her.

Sad to say, this most precious and sublime feature of the Yosemite National Park, one of the greatest of all our natural resources for the uplifting joy and peace and health of the people, is in danger of being dammed and made into a reservoir to help supply San Francisco with water and light, thus flooding it from wall to wall and burying its gardens and groves one or two hundred feet deep. This grossly destructive commercial scheme has long been planned and urged (though water as pure and abundant can be got from sources outside of the people's park, in a dozen different places), because of the comparative cheapness of the dam and of the territory which it is sought to divert from the great uses to which it was dedicated in the Act of 1890 establishing the Yosemite National Park.

The making of gardens and parks goes on with civilization all over the world, and they increase both in

[4] *Pteridium.*

size and number as their value is recognized. Everybody needs beauty as well as bread, places to play in and pray in, where Nature may heal and cheer and give strength to body and soul alike. This natural beauty-hunger is made manifest in the little window-sill gardens of the poor, though perhaps only a geranium slip in a broken cup, as well as in the carefully tended rose and lily gardens of the rich, the thousands of spacious city parks and botanical gardens, and in our magnificent National Parks—the Yellowstone, Yosemite, Sequoia, etc.—Nature's sublime wonderlands, the admiration and joy of the world. Nevertheless, like anything else worth while, from the very beginning, however well guarded, they have always been subject to attack by despoiling gain-seekers and mischief-makers of every degree from Satan to Senators, eagerly trying to make everything immediately and selfishly commercial, with schemes disguised in smug-smiling philanthropy, industriously, sham-piously crying, "Conservation, conservation, panutilization," that man and beast may be fed and the dear Nation made great. Thus long ago a few enterprising merchants utilized the Jerusalem temple as a place of business instead of a place of prayer, changing money, buying and selling cattle and sheep and doves; and earlier still, the first forest reservation, including only one tree, was likewise despoiled. Ever since the establishment of the Yosemite National Park, strife has been going on around its borders and I suppose this will go on as part of the universal battle between right and wrong, however much its boundaries may be shorn, or its wild beauty destroyed.

The first application to the Government by the San Francisco Supervisors for the commercial use of Lake Eleanor and the Hetch Hetchy Valley was made in 1903, and on December 22nd of that year it was denied by the Secretary of the Interior, Mr. Hitchcock, who truthfully said:

> Presumably the Yosemite National Park was created such by law because of the natural objects of varying degrees of scenic importance located within its boundaries, inclusive alike of its beautiful small lakes, like Eleanor, and its majestic wonders, like Hetch Hetchy and Yosemite Valley. It is the aggregation of such natural scenic features that makes the Yosemite Park a wonderland which the Congress of the United States sought by law to reserve for all coming time as nearly as practicable in the condition fashioned by the hand of the Creator—a worthy object of National pride and a source of healthful pleasure and rest for the thousands of people who may annually sojourn there during the heated months.

In 1907 when Mr. Garfield became Secretary of the Interior the application was renewed and granted; but under his successor, Mr. Fisher, the matter has been referred to a Commission, which as this volume goes to press still has it under consideration.

The most delightful and wonderful camp-grounds in the Park are its three great valleys—Yosemite, Hetch Hetchy, and Upper Tuolumne; and they are also the most important places with reference to their positions relative to the other great features—the Merced and Tuolumne Canyons, and the High Sierra peaks and glaciers, etc., at the head of the rivers. The main part of the Tuolumne Valley is a spacious flowery lawn four or five miles long, surrounded by magnificent snowy mountains, slightly separated from other beautiful meadows, which together make a series about twelve miles in length, the highest reaching to the feet of Mount Dana, Mount Gibbs, Mount Lyell and Mount

McClure. It is about 8500 feet above the sea, and forms the grand central High Sierra camp-ground from which excursions are made to the noble mountains, domes, glaciers, etc.; across the Range to the Mono Lake and volcanoes and down the Tuolumne Canyon to Hetch Hetchy. Should Hetch Hetchy be submerged for a reservoir, as proposed, not only would it be utterly destroyed, but the sublime canyon way to the heart of the High Sierra would be hopelessly blocked and the great camping-ground, as the watershed of a city drinking system, virtually would be closed to the public. So far as I have learned, few of all the thousands who have seen the park and seek rest and peace in it are in favor of this outrageous scheme.

One of my later visits to the Valley was made in the autumn of 1907 with the late William Keith, the artist. The leaf-colors were then ripe, and the great god-like rocks in repose seemed to glow with life. The artist, under their spell, wandered day after day along the river and through the groves and gardens, studying the wonderful scenery; and, after making about forty sketches, declared with enthusiasm that although its walls were less sublime in height, in picturesque beauty and charm Hetch Hetchy surpassed even Yosemite.

That anyone would try to destroy such a place seems incredible; but sad experience shows that there are people good enough and bad enough for anything. The proponents of the dam scheme bring forward a lot of bad arguments to prove that the only righteous thing to do with the people's parks is to destroy them bit by bit as they are able. Their arguments are curiously like those of the devil, devised for the destruction of the first garden—so much of the very best Eden fruit going to waste; so much of the best Tuolumne water and Tuolumne scenery going to waste. Few of their statements are even partly true, and all are misleading.

Thus, Hetch Hetchy, they say, is a "low-lying meadow." On the contrary, it is a high-lying natural landscape garden, as the photographic illustrations show.

"It is a common minor feature, like thousands of others." On the contrary it is a very uncommon feature; after Yosemite, the rarest and in many ways the most important in the National Park.

"Damming and submerging it 175 feet deep would enhance its beauty by forming a crystal-clear lake." Landscape gardens, places of recreation and worship, are never made beautiful by destroying and burying them. The beautiful sham lake, forsooth, would be only an eyesore, a dismal blot on the landscape, like many others to be seen in the Sierra. For, instead of keeping it at the same level all the year, allowing Nature centuries of time to make new shores, it would, of course, be full only a month or two in the spring, when the snow is melting fast; then it would be gradually drained, exposing the slimy sides of the basin and shallower parts of the bottom, with the gathered drift and waste, death and decay of the upper basins, caught here instead of being swept on to decent natural burial along the banks of the river or in the sea. Thus the Hetch Hetchy dam-lake would be only a rough imitation of a natural lake for a few of the spring months, an open sepulcher for the others.

"Hetch Hetchy water is the purest of all to be found in the Sierra, unpolluted, and forever unpollutable." On the contrary, excepting that of the Merced below Yosemite, it is less pure than that of most of the other Sierra streams, because of the sewerage of campgrounds draining into it, especially of the Big Tuolumne Meadows camp-ground, occupied by hundreds of tourists and mountaineers, with their animals, for months every summer, soon to be followed by thousands from all the world.

These temple destroyers, devotees of ravaging commercialism, seem to have a perfect contempt for Nature, and, instead of lifting their eyes to the God of the mountains, lift them to the Almighty Dollar.

Dam Hetch Hetchy! As well dam for water-tanks the people's cathedrals and churches, for no holier temple has ever been consecrated by the heart of man.[5]

[5] When the Raker Act was passed by Congress and signed by President Woodrow Wilson in December, 1913, Muir had lost his long campaign to preserve Hetch Hetchy Valley. The City of San Francisco began construction activities the next year. O'Shaughnessy Dam was completed and water storage commenced in 1923. The reservoir fills the former valley and backs into the canyon above, fluctuating seasonally. Public access by auto ends at the dam, and promised recreational facilities have never been developed.

APPENDIX A

LEGISLATION ABOUT THE YOSEMITE

In the year 1864, Congress passed the following act:—

ACT OF JUNE 30, 1864 (13 STAT., 325).

AN ACT Authorizing a grant to the State of California of the "Yo-Semite Valley," and of the land embracing the "Mariposa Big Tree Grove."

"Be it enacted by the Senate and House of Representatives of the United States of America, in Congress assembled, That there shall be, and is hereby, granted to the State of California, the 'Cleft' or 'Gorge' in the Granite Peak of the Sierra Nevada Mountains, situated in the county of Mariposa, in the State aforesaid, and the headwaters of the Merced River, and known as the Yosemite Valley, with its branches and spurs, in estimated length fifteen miles, and in average width one mile back from the main edge of the precipice, on each side of the Valley, with the stipulation, nevertheless, that the said State shall accept this grant upon the express conditions that the premises shall be held for public use, resort, and recreation; shall be inalienable for all time; but leases not exceeding ten years may be granted for portions of said premises. All incomes derived from leases of privileges to be expended in the preservation and improvement of the property, or the roads leading thereto; the boundaries to be established at the cost of said State by the United States Surveyor-General of California, whose official plat, when affirmed by the Commissioner of the General Land Office, shall constitute the evidence of the locus, extent, and limits of the said Cleft or Gorge; the premises to be managed by the

Governor of the State, with eight other Commissioners, to be appointed by the Executive of California, and who shall receive no compensation for their services.

"SEC. 2. *And be it further enacted,* That there shall likewise be, and there is hereby, granted to the said State of California, the tracts embracing what is known as the 'Mariposa Big Tree Grove,' not to exceed the area of four sections, and to be taken in legal subdivisions of one-quarter section each, with the like stipulations as expressed in the first section of this Act as to the State's acceptance, with like conditions as in the first section of this Act as to inalienability, yet with the same lease privileges; the income to be expended in the preservation, improvement, and protection of the property, the premises to be managed by Commissioners, as stipulated in the first section of this Act, and to be taken in legal subdivisions as aforesaid; and the official plat of the United States Surveyor-General, when affirmed by the Commissioner of the General Land Office, to be the evidence of the locus of the said Mariposa Big Tree Grove."

This important act was approved by the President, June 30, 1864, and shortly after the Governor of California, F. F. Low, issued a proclamation taking possession of the Yosemite Valley and Mariposa Grove of Big Trees, in the name and on behalf of the State, appointing commissioners to manage them, and warning all persons against trespassing or settling there without authority, and especially forbidding the cutting of timber and other injurious acts.

The first Board of Commissioners were F. Law Olmsted, J. D. Whitney, William Ashburner, I. W. Raymond, E. S. Holden, Alexander Deering, George W. Coulter, and Galen Clark.

ACT OF OCTOBER 1, 1890 (26 STAT., 650).[1]

AN ACT To set apart certain tracts of land in the State of California as forest reservations.

"Be it enacted by the Senate and House of Representatives of the United States of America in Congress assembled, That the tracts of land in the State of California known as described as follows: Commencing at the northwest corner of township two north, range nineteen east Mount Diablo meridian, thence eastwardly on the line between townships two and three north, ranges twenty-four and twenty-five east; thence southwardly on the line between ranges twenty-four and twenty-five east to the Mount Diablo base line; thence eastwardly on said base line to the corner to township one south, ranges twenty-five and twenty-six east; thence southwardly on the line between ranges twenty-five and twenty-six east to the southeast corner of township two south, range twenty-five east; thence eastwardly on the line between townships two and three south, range twenty-six east to the corner to townships two and three south, ranges twenty-six and twenty-seven east; thence southwardly on the line between ranges twenty-six and twenty-seven east to the first standard parallel south; thence westwardly on the first standard parallel south to the southwest corner of township four south, range nineteen east; thence northwardly on the line between ranges eighteen and nineteen east to the northwest corner of township two south, range nineteen east; thence westwardly on the line between townships one and two south to the southwest corner of township one south, range nineteen east; thence northwardly on the line between ranges eighteen and nineteen east to the northwest corner of township two north, range nineteen east, the place of beginning, are hereby reserved and withdrawn from settlement, occupancy, or sale under the laws of the United States, and

[1] Sections 1 and 2 of this act pertain to the Yosemite National Park, while section 3 sets apart General Grant National Park, and also a portion of Sequoia National Park.

set apart as reserved forest lands; and all persons who shall locate or settle upon, or occupy the same or any part thereof, except as hereinafter provided, shall be considered trespassers and removed therefrom: *Provided, however,* That nothing in this act shall be construed as in anywise affecting the grant of lands made to the State of California by virtue of the act entitled, 'An act authorizing a grant to the State of California of the Yosemite Valley, and of the land embracing the Mariposa Big-Tree Grove, appeared June thirtieth, eighteen hundred and sixty-four; or as affecting any bona-fide entry of land made within the limits above described under any law of the United States prior to the approval of this act.

"SEC. 2. That said reservation shall be under the exclusive control of the Secretary of the Interior, whose duty it shall be, as soon as practicable, to make and publish such rules and regulations as he may deem necessary or proper for the care and management of the same. Such regulations shall provide for the preservation from injury of all timber, mineral deposits, natural curiosities, or wonders within said reservation, and their retention in their natural condition. The Secretary may, in his discretion, grant leases for building purposes for terms not exceeding ten years of small parcels of ground not exceeding five acres; at such places in said reservation as shall require the erection of buildings for the accommodation of visitors; all of the proceeds of said leases and other revenues that may be derived from any source connected with said reservation to be expended under his direction in the management of the same and the construction of roads and paths therein. He shall provide against the wanton destruction of the fish, and game found within said reservation, and against their capture or destruction, for the purposes of merchandise or profit. He shall also cause all persons trespassing upon the same after the passage of this act to be removed therefrom, and, generally, shall be authorized to take all such measures as shall be necessary or proper to fully carry out the objects and purposes of this act.

"SEC. 3. There shall also be and is hereby reserved and

withdrawn from settlement, occupancy, or sale under the laws of the United States, and shall be set apart as reserved forest lands, as hereinbefore provided, and subject to all the limitations and provisions herein contained, the following additional lands, to wit: Township seventeen south, range thirty east of the Mount Diablo meridian, excepting sections thirty-one, thirty-two, thirty-three, and thirty-four of said township, included in a previous bill. And there is also reserved and withdrawn from settlement, occupancy, or sale under the laws of the United States, and set apart as forest lands, subject to like limitations, conditions, and provisions, all of townships fifteen and sixteen south, of ranges twenty-nine and thirty east of the Mount Diablo meridian. And there is also hereby reserved and withdrawn from settlement, occupancy, or sale under the laws of the United States, and set apart as reserved forest lands under like limitations, restrictions, and provisions, sections five and six in township fourteen south, range twenty-eight east of Mount Diablo meridian, and also sections thirty-one and thirty-two of township thirteen south, range twenty-eight east of the same meridian. Nothing in this act shall authorize rules or contracts touching the protection and improvement of said reservations, beyond the sums that may be received by the Secretary of the Interior under the foregoing provisions, or authorize any charge against the Treasury of the United States."

ACT OF THE LEGISLATURE OF THE STATE OF CALIFORNIA, APPROVED MARCH 3, 1905

"SEC. 1. The State of California does hereby recede and regrant unto the United States of America the 'cleft' or 'gorge' in the granite peak of the Sierra Nevada Mountains, situated in the county of Mariposa, State of California, and the headwaters of the Merced River, and known as the Yosemite Valley, with its branches and spurs, granted unto the State of California in trust for public use, resort, and recreation by the act of Congress entitled, 'An act authorizing a grant to the State of California of the Yosemite

Valley and of the land embracing the Mariposa Big Tree Grove,' approved June thirtieth, eighteen hundred and sixty-four; and the State of California does hereby relinquish unto the United States of America and resign the trusts created and granted by the said act of Congress.

"SEC. 2. The State of California does hereby recede and regrant unto the United States of America the tracts embracing what is known as the 'Mariposa Big Tree Grove,' granted unto the State of California in trust for public use, resort, and recreation by the act of Congress referred to in section one of this act, and the State of California does hereby relinquish unto the United States of America and resign the trusts created and granted by the said act of Congress.

"SEC. 3. This act shall take effect from and after acceptance by the United States of America of the recessions and regrants herein made, thereby forever releasing the State of California from further cost of maintaining the said premises, the same to be held for all time by the United States of America for public use, resort, and recreation, and imposing on the United States of America the cost of maintaining the same as a national park: *Provided, however,* That the recession and regrant hereby made shall not affect vested rights and interests of third persons."[2]

[2] Keystone of legislative protection is the National Park Act of 1916. It sets forth the purpose of the National Park System: "to conserve the scenery and the natural and historic objects and the wild life therein and to provide for the enjoyment of the same in such manner and by such means as will leave them unimpaired for the enjoyment of future generations." The campaign of Muir and others to save Hetch Hetchy was lost, but it contributed to this fundamental victory for park conservation.

APPENDIX B

TABLE OF DISTANCES

From the Guardian's office, in the village,[1] the distances to various points are in miles as follows:

	Miles
Bridal Veil Fall	4.04
Cascade Falls	7.67
Clouds Rest, Summit	11.81
Columbia Rock, on Eagle Peak Trail	1.98
Dana, Mt., Summit	40.34
Eagle Peak	6.59
El Capitan Bridge	3.63
Glacier Point, direct trail	4.45
Glacier Point, by Nevada Fall	16.98
Lyell, Mt., Summit	38.20
Merced Bridge	2.03
Mirror Lake, by Hunt's avenue	2.91
Nevada Fall (Hotel)[2]	4.63
Nevada Fall, Bridge above	5.45
Pohono Bridge	5.29
Register Rock	3.24
Ribbon Fall	3.99
Rocky Point (base of Three Brothers)	1.45
Tenaya Creek Bridge	2.26
Tenaya Lake	16.00

[1] The Guardian's office during the administration of Yosemite Valley by the State of California was located downstream from Sentinel Bridge and later in the Old Village. Columbia Rock is on the Yosemite Falls Trail. Merced Bridge may have been in the vicinity of Happy Isles. Register Rock is at the junction of Mist Trail and the horse trail on the Vernal Fall route. Mileages in this table have not been corrected. Consult maps and rangers.

[2] A hotel, Casa Nevada, was formerly located near the foot of Nevada Fall, on the north side of the Merced.

	Miles
Yosemite Falls, foot	0.90
Yosemite Falls, foot Upper Fall	2.67
Yosemite Falls, top	4.33
Soda Springs (Eagle Peak Trail)	24.50
Sentinel Dome	5.57
Union Point, on Glacier Point Trail	3.13
Vernal Fall	3.50

APPENDIX C

MAXIMUM RATES FOR TRANSPORTATION[1]

The following rates for transportation in and about the Valley have been established by the Board of Commissioners:

SADDLE-HORSES

From	Route to	Amount
Valley	Glacier Point and Sentinel Dome, and return, direct, same day	$3 00
Valley	Glacier Point, Sentinel Dome, and Fissures, and return, direct, same day	3 75
Valley	Glacier Point, Sentinel Dome, and Fissures, passing night at Glacier Point	3 00
Valley	Glacier Point, Sentinel Dome, Nevada Fall, and Casa Nevada, passing night at Casa Nevada	3 00
Valley	Glacier Point, Sentinel Dome, Nevada Fall, Vernal Fall, and thence to Valley same day	4 00
Glacier Point	Valley direct	2 00
Glacier Point	Sentinel Dome, Nevada Fall, and Casa Nevada, passing night at Casa Nevada	2 00

[1] The interest of this section is historical and nostalgic. Most visitors to Yosemite are now motorized, but saddle horses and bicycles are rented, and there are sight-seeing buses. For information, write to Yosemite Park and Curry Co., Yosemite National Park, California. At the Park, consult the Yosemite Transportation System.

MAXIMUM RATES FOR TRANSPORTATION—
Continued.

From	Route to	Amount
Glacier Point	Sentinel Dome, Nevada Fall, Vernal Fall, and thence to Valley same day	$3 00
Valley	Summits, Vernal and Nevada Falls, direct, and return to Valley same day	3 00
Valley	Glacier Point by Casa Nevada, passing night at Glacier Point	3 00
Valley	Summits, Vernal and Nevada Falls, Sentinel Dome, Glacier Point, and thence to Valley same day	4 00
Valley	Clouds Rest and return to Casa Nevada	3 00
Valley	Clouds Rest and return to Valley same day	5 00
Casa Nevada	Clouds Rest and return to Casa Nevada or Valley same day	3 00
Casa Nevada	Valley direct	2 00
Casa Nevada	Nevada Fall, Sentinel Dome, and Glacier Point, passing night at Glacier Point	2 00
Valley	Nevada Fall, Sentinel Dome, Glacier Point, and Valley same day	3 00
	Upper Yosemite Fall, Eagle Peak, and return	3 00
	Charge for guide (including horse), when furnished	3 00
	Saddle-horses, on level of Valley, per day	2 50

1. The above charges do not include feed for horses when passing night at Casa Nevada or Glacier Point.

2. Where Valley is specified as starting-point, the above rates prevail from any hotel in Valley, or from the foot of any trail.

3. Any shortening of above trips, without proportionate reduction of rates, shall be at the option of those hiring horses.

4. Trips other than those above specified shall be subject to special arrangement between letter and hirer.

CARRIAGES

From	Route to	Amount
Hotels	Mirror Lake and return, direct	$1 00
Hotels	Mirror Lake and return by Tissiack Avenue	1 25
Hotels	Mirror Lake and return to foot of Trail, to Vernal and Nevada Falls	1 00
Hotels	Bridal Veil Fall and return, direct	1 00
Hotels	Pohono Bridge, down either side of Valley, and return on opposite side, stopping at Yosemite and Bridal Veil Falls	1 50
Hotels	Cascade Falls, down either side of Valley, and return on opposite side, stopping at Yosemite and Bridal Veil Falls	2 25
Hotels	Artist Point and return, direct, stopping at Bridal Veil Fall	2 00
Hotels	New Inspiration Point and return, direct, stopping at Bridal Veil Fall	2 00
	Grand Round Drive, including Yosemite and Bridal Veil Falls, excluding Lake and Cascades	2 50
	Grand Round Drive, including Yosemite and Bridal Veil Falls, Lake, and Cascades	3 50

1. When the value of the seats hired in any vehicle shall exceed $15 for a two-horse team, or $25 for a four-horse team, *for any trip* in the above schedule, the persons hiring the seats shall have the privilege of paying no more than the aggregate sums of $15 and $25 *per trip* for a two-horse and four-horse team, respectively.

2. If saddle-horses should be substituted for any of the above carriage trips, carriage rates will apply to each horse. In no case shall the *per diem* charge of $2.50 for each saddle-horse, on level of Valley, be exceeded.

Any excess of the above rates, as well as *any* extortion, incivility, misrepresentation, or the riding of unsafe animals, should be promptly reported at the Guardian's office.

Books and Maps for Readers of *The Yosemite*

BY JOHN MUIR

The Mountains of California (N.Y.: Century Company, 1894; enlarged edition, 1911. Doubleday Anchor Book N12, 1961.)

My First Summer in the Sierra (Boston: Houghton Mifflin Company, 1911.)

Our National Parks (Boston: Houghton Mifflin Company, 1901.)

John of the Mountains (edited from Muir's unpublished journals by Linnie Marsh Wolfe. Boston: Houghton Mifflin Company, 1938.)

Yosemite and the High Sierra (selections from Muir's works edited by Charlotte E. Mauk, with photographs by Ansel Adams. Boston: Houghton Mifflin Company, 1948.)

John Muir's Studies in the Sierra (edited by William E. Colby. San Francisco: Sierra Club, revised edition, 1960.)

FROM THE U. S. GEOLOGICAL SURVEY

Topographic Map of Yosemite National Park (scale 1/125,000; includes Dardanelles, Bridgeport, Yosemite and Mt. Lyell quadrangles.)

Topographic Map of Yosemite Valley (scale 1/24,000.)

Geologic History of the Yosemite Valley (U.S.G.S. Professional Paper 160, by François E. Matthes. Washington, D.C.: 1930.)

FROM THE SIERRA CLUB

Starr's Guide to the John Muir Trail and the High Sierra Region, by Walter A. Starr, Jr. (Eighth edition, 1962.)

A Climber's Guide to the High Sierra (edited by Hervey
   Voge, fourth printing, 1962.)
Going Light—with Backpack or Burro (edited by David R.
   Brower, sixth printing, 1960.)

FROM THE NATIONAL PARK SERVICE

Yosemite National Park, California (informational bro-
   chure.)

FROM THE YOSEMITE NATURAL HISTORY ASSOCIATION

Yosemite Nature Notes (self-guiding tour booklets for
   the Park and for certain areas, and handbooks on birds,
   fishes, mammals, trees, flowers, geology, etc.)
Books for children (*Animal Friends of the Sierra, A Day
   with Tupi.*)

ALSO RECOMMENDED

My Camera in Yosemite Valley, by Ansel Adams (Yosem-
   ite: Virginia Adams; Boston: Houghton Mifflin Com-
   pany, 1949.)
One Hundred Years in Yosemite, by Carl P. Russell
   (Berkeley and Los Angeles: University of California
   Press, revised 1947.)

NOTE

To obtain publications, write:
   U. S. Geological Survey, Federal Center, Denver, Col-
      orado, or Washington 25, D.C.
   Sierra Club, 1050 Mills Tower, San Francisco 4, Cal-
      ifornia.
   Superintendent of Documents, U. S. Government Print-
      ing Office, Washington 25, D.C. (for Park brochure).
   Yosemite Natural History Association, Yosemite Na-
      tional Park, California.

INDEX